Aurea Vidyā Collection*

———— 21 ————

* For a complete list of titles see page 237.

This book was originally published in Italian as *La Filosofia dell'Essere* and later as *Quale Democrazia?* by Associazione Ecoculturale Parmenides (formerly Edizioni Āśram Vidyā). Rome, Italy

First Published in English in 2019 by
Aurea Vidyā
39 West 88th Street
New York, NY 10024

All Rights © Āśram Vidyā
Via Azone 20 – 00165 Rome, Italy

The proceeds from this book – to which there are no Author's rights – will be used for reprints. The contents of this book may not be reproduced in any form without the written permission of the publisher, except for the quotation of brief passages in criticism, by citing the source.

ISBN 978-1-931406-27-7

Library of Congress Control Number: 2019912995

On the cover: Summer Solstice from 88th Street and Columbus Avenue. NYC.

Raphael
Āśram Vidyā Order

THE PHILOSOPHY OF BEING

A conception of life for coming out of
the turmoil of individual and social conflict

Aurea Vidyā

CONTENTS

Preface   9

FIRST PART

Projection/Idol   15
The Social Orders   47
Ultimate Freedom   79
Peace and Class Co-operation   95
Following One's Own Duty   109
Transcending Discursive Thought   119
Philosophy of Being   127
Traditional Art   139

SECOND PART

Shadows Cast on Gurus and on Traditional Culturalists   161
Scourgers and Executioners   171
Initiation and Rite   179
Solution of the Energetic Compound   189
Glossary   223
About Raphael   231

PREFACE

A few years ago some people belonging to different ideological groups, yet also having realisative urges, found themselves united by the same pressing questions: can social politics, as generally understood, solve the fundamental problems of the individual, really iron out disparities at the social level, and lead humanity to peaceful co-operation and well-being? Are the political ideologies of the world of becoming, with their underlying motivations, truly valid? And further more, can there be a social philosophy which is able to deal with the psycho-spiritual urges of the individual as well as the contingent, material demands of social politics?

Although such problems were not connected to the teaching imparted by Raphael, the urgent nature of the need was such that he agreed to consider a series of questions, of an impersonal nature, with the prospect of being able to answer them satisfactorily.

At Raphael's suggestion, the group was augmented by people with exclusively realisative urges and a predisposition towards *Advaita Vedānta, Asparśavāda*, and *Platonism*.

The discussion, held on a number of occasions, required a great deal of time, and the topics covered were many and varied. Some of the questions are so outspoken and forceful that they sometimes smack of aggressiveness; but this is because some members of the group have had some negative experiences in the socio-political sphere and also in the spiritual and traditional realm.

All the participants agreed that a change was necessary, but what kind of change? And which direction should the committed energy follow?

We have chosen those questions and answers which we feel are useful for the reader.

Although we don't feel we are divulging the essence or conclusion, we may still stress that Raphael considers politics, as generally understood, to be a dialectical moment of *individuality* and, as such, must have its own validity and *raison d'être*.

In some Eastern and Western ideologies there are truths which are undoubtedly valid, but which people, through lack of self-realisation, fail to put into practice, and actually fabricate excuses not to do so.

So many revolutions, past and present, although they have been born from just motivations and have praiseworthy plans, are betrayed by the revolutionaries themselves once they have gained power. All this becomes clear from the answers given by Raphael, as does the fact that Raphael indicates a vision of *politics* which does not derive from the passionate ego.

The Philosophy of Being, when it is adapted to the political order, is that Philosophy which proposes a radical transformation, not in effects but in causes. This implies that, if there has to be a revolution, it will transform the individual himself, that is, it will transform him inwardly rather than outwardly.

Whether in good faith or bad, to speak of social revolution rather than of mental transformation indicates an unwillingness to put the true and ultimate revolution into effect. In other words, it indicates an unwillingness to change anything at all.

Here is another point to consider: when Raphael speaks of *Philosophia perennis*, traditional Metaphysics, and so on, he is referring to that Philosophy of Being which is a result not of the individualised mind but of noetic contemplation. This philosophical Tradition, therefore, does not represent the cultural tradition of a people, their customs, their ideological or formal conservatism, or even their institutionalised and dogmatic religious element.

The philosophy of which Raphael speaks has its origin in the Principle and extends as far as the human being. Thus it transcends 'party politics', 'religious sectarianism', and cultural/scientific divisions, just as it transcends all egoistic interest, be it individual, national, or racial.

Every sort of conservatism, institutional and otherwise, has its origin in the spirit of preservation pertaining to the conflicting ego and is consequently opposed to the Philosophy of Being. So if there are a number of references to Śaṅkara's *Advaita Vedānta*, Gauḍapāda's *Asparśavāda*, or to Plato and Plotinus, it is because these traditional teachings belong to realisative Metaphysics, or, rather, are Metaphysics, which means that they are outside every framework of emotional religious fanaticism and thus beyond all irrational and exclusivist bias. In fact, the content of Raphael's replies bears mainly upon the philosophy of Plato, Plotinus, and other Neo-Platonists, that is, upon the Western Mystery Tradition.

In the course of the discussion some concepts are repeated, but this is because the questions that are put on different occasions make it necessary. In addition, some questions and answers could have been transposed to more appropriate chapters, but it was felt better to leave the discussion as it actually unfolded, without changing the sequence.

In accordance with the wishes of the Group, we would like to express our gratitude to Raphael for agreeing to consider themes which are not, strictly speaking, an integral part of his nature as an *asparśin*.

Āśram Vidyā

'*Finis totius et partis esse potest et multiplex, scilicet propinquus et remotus; sed, omissa subtili investigatione, dicendum est breviter quod finis totius et partis est removere viventes in hac vita de statu miserie et perducere ad statum felicitatis.*'

'The aim of the whole and of the part could be manifold: both near and far. But putting aside a close consideration, it could be briefly said that the aim of the whole and of the part is to remove beings, in their life, from the state of misery and take them to the state of happiness.'

Letter written by Dante to Can Grande della Scala

PROJECTION/IDOL

Q.[1] Can you tell me what makes people hold on to certain ideologies? What impels them to identify with their concepts? How do people find certainty in a political or religious ideology, or in a scientific theory? I mean, why is the individual driven to *believe* himself to be an objectified image?

R. To understand this state of affairs, we need to briefly consider the dynamics of the empirical representative mind.

The mind operates through images and projections, because it adopts a twofold attitude[2] when facing any datum. When we perceive a tree, the mind tries to *imagine* the reality/tree, and, by making use of its memories and its correlations with other data, it creates a *concept* of what the tree is. But the concept is constructed on the data supplied by the five senses. Usually the consciousness holds to this and identifies itself so fully with the concept that it creates an identity with it.

We may define this kind of perception/knowledge as one of relationship, subject and object, description, and so on. To imagine a datum is one thing; to *know it* is

---

[1] Q is for Questioner. R is for Raphael. + is for the person who has put the preceding question.

[2] For a deeper understanding of this aspect, see 'The limits of the mind' and 'Subject and Object' in *At the Source of Life*, by Raphael. Aurea Vidyā, New York.

another. Moreover, the ego needs to believe in something in order to stay alive, and the imaginative mind provides it with the basic material for survival.

When the individual seeks to solve his existential/social problems, what does he do? He projects an image which he calls 'politics' and which frequently takes form as an ideology and a 'party'; and he qualifies it according to his particular urges and aspirations. Slowly a great effigy takes shape, the *political goddess*, and he rests all his expectations upon this goddess. In truth, it is the birth of an idol, which, as we know, can be exalted to the point of fanaticism.

In the course of time, the aspirations of the masses have been placed in the advent of a Messiah, the coming of the Kingdom of Heaven, the arrival of a Superman, science, industrialisation, bureaucratic power, democracy, dictatorship and so on. But these 'advents' are merely projections, images full of expectations and thaumaturgical powers. When the idol fails to live up to these expectations, the mind turns against it and tries to bring it low, often with the use of force.

Wherever there are idols and images to worship, you have idolatry. Idols, created by the out-going and projecting mind, are drugs which befuddle the awareness of the being. Men can be put to sleep by the power of an idol which has been patiently constructed by *prepared minds*.

We may cite a very significant statement made by the German physicist C. F. von Weizsacker on the occasion of the bi-centenary of a pharmaceutical association in Basel: 'Today science is the only thing in which everyone believes: it is the only universal religion of our time. ... The scientist has thus put himself into an ambiguous position: he is the priest of this new religion, he knows its secrets and its wonders; what others find disconcerting, strange, or secret is clear for him.'

It is inevitable that as long as the mind puts its salvation outside itself, the ego 'gets by' and perpetuates itself; as long as the hoarding, acquisitive, and reactive ego persists, there is no system of politics or science which can grant salvation. The ego cannot survive without an idol: it is subject to the idol and does everything in its name. The qualities attributed to the idol have little to do with the actual level of awareness of the projecting being, which is passively waiting for the idol to work miracles. This means that, by being subservient to the image we have made, we communicate with ourselves in an *alienated* way.

If on the one hand we have fashioned the idol/miracle, on the other hand the idol imprisons us. This is the paradox of the individual who makes images.

Many people invest the idol with qualities of social justice, brotherhood, order, and so on, but the operative *subject* does not experience these qualities in himself, and cannot experience them, because he has projected them, thereby becoming alienated. Many actually cause a revolution in order to change things, to create justice, social equality, and the like. Once they have gained power, these same people who have fought to abolish injustice now commit as much injustice as their predecessors did, albeit in different forms. This happens because they have projected an *image* of revolution, which is the result, among other things, of a merely emotional reaction, without being, or embodying, the essence of the revolution. We run after our projections, our idols, our ghosts, without ever catching them, for the simple reason that we always put them in *front* of us.

+ So we need to acknowledge that the individual is obliged to create institutions because, having alienated himself, he can no longer live under his own steam. Having projected the goddess of justice, he must necessarily build law-courts. Yet these institutions cannot meet his need, his 'lack', his deprivation, can they?

R. Until *we ourselves are* filled through and through with justice, order, and composure, we shall never be able to triumph over social injustice. Those institutions are always presided over by 'deficient' beings.

Q. Then the individual not only creates the gods in his own image, but politics and science as well. Is that correct?

R. Politics is a very powerful idol, or fetish, which has millions of devotees, faithful followers, and even fanatics. And just as people have killed each other in the name of the Love of Christ, for example, so vile and irrational crimes are committed in the name of justice and social progress. All the roads of the philosophy of becoming lead to the same end: alienation. This world has no outside, no other place, towards which the philosophy of becoming can direct it. The progressivists and the conservatives, although they use power in different ways, share a common destiny: that of alienation.

We have referred to the other idol, which is science with its 'progress'. Everything is demanded of science. It is thought of as a power which can do everything, which can solve everything; and when this doesn't happen, its devotees, losing trust, turn against it. Nowadays, for example, many people who belong to particular socio-political groups no longer believe in science. The image that they had *projected* of science was that it could solve the problems of humanity with its conception of progress, its technological developments, and its extra-planetary discoveries; but this hasn't happened, and so they have rebelled.

As long as we live on projections and idols, we shall be unable to re-establish justice, equality, and fraternity, because these are not to be expressed through an idol but lived by our own consciousness.

When we are fully united with Love, Harmony, and Accord, which at certain levels are participation and sharing, then the age of justice will be able to prevail in society.

According to the Philosophy of Being, the *Philosophia perennis* which comes forth from the Principle, the fundamental human *problem* resides in the actual consciousness of the being; only by going back into itself does it discover the power to realise peace, harmony, and well-being. In other words, it can be certain of its own completeness; to look for it outside, to project the idols of science, politics, religion (as generally understood), liberty, and equality means postponing the solution to the problem.

In saying this, one has no desire to disregard the function of science, politics, religion, and so on, especially in an insane alienated society. On the other hand, this is not our thought. We regard these things as channels through which the inner Reality may be expressed at certain levels of existence. But when we elevate the instrument, the means of expression or the channel to the position of an idol, deity, or fetish, through our accompanying submission and fanatical worship, then we overturn the truth of things. 'The Sabbath was made for man, not man for the Sabbath.'

Q. Why does the individual look outside for something that is within him? What drives him to rely on things and not on himself?

R. Let's go back to the previous question. A great deal depends on the nature of the mind, which tends to go outwards and manifest itself objectively; besides, this is its function. Every instrument, or body, manifests specific qualifications. The mental body – and therefore the most relevant part of individuality – expresses itself in this way; it has the characteristic of putting the experienced event outside itself.

For the empirical individual what is real is *what is facing him*, that is, the object which is projected; and although he may see it vanish a moment later, he still views it as just as real. Not being able, or not wishing, to conceive of other possibilities expressive of reality, he is forced to recognise as real that which becomes, that which fundamentally exists and does not exist. The greater the identification with what is thought, the greater the objectivisation.

Apart from any political colouring, objective materialism takes its rise from this attitude of mind. It says that reality is that objective, the material object which *faces us*, the *other*. If it then reaches down to the realm of politics, it considers reality to be material well-being, production, what is mere consumer goods.

In truth, once the individual places reality outside himself, he not only lives a life of subjugation and alienation, but he also finds that reality itself is constantly elusive and unattainable. It is similar to what happens at the dog-racing track: to make the dog run, a piece of meat is put in front of him. The dog runs, but so does the piece of meat, which is attached to the rotating arm to which the dog is tied. The wheel of becoming keeps turning as long as the individual places outside of himself that which is within himself. All who wake up to this acknowledgement begin to slow down and finally come to a stop. This is the moment of return to Source, return to Being. One who has understood the *game* no longer plays, but lets the game continue for the sake of those who still need to play it.

+ I believe some politicians might be opposed to the Philosophy of Being because it forces them to acknowledge that the reality rests in the hearts of men and not in the idols which they have patiently and diabolically constructed.

If, as is often said, religion can be the opium of the people, then politics can be a drug which turns millions of people into sleep-walkers.

However that may be, what position does the mind need to be in to rise above itself?

R. One of silence, of listening. But we have to be very careful when we speak of silence.

There are many who imagine that they have to deaden all the senses, become passive, and stop thinking. Others believe that they have to deny themselves so completely that they lose their sensitivity and even their judgement. We have said that the function of the mind is to move by projecting and dragging the consciousness to identify with its projections. Now we must gradually gain control of the thinking *movement* and then bring about *detachment* from the projections or images that are conceived.

Control of the mental movement and subsequent *detachment*[1] from the products of our thought constitute the preliminary aim of every serious spiritual discipline (*sādhanā*). As we may note, what is necessary is to sever the 'Seer' from what is thought, projected, and observed.

To effect this process, it is not irrational passivity that is required, but greater vigilance, greater will-power, a greater sense of balance, and a greater centrality of consciousness.

With regard, then, to what you said at the beginning of your question, remember that we are referring to a politician who has subjugated himself to the idol. Of course, we have to distinguish a politician from a Politician.

Q. From what we are saying, I have to conclude that there are two reasons why man projects outside himself the image of the Prince[2]: the first is that it is in his nature to project the Saviour; the second is that, failing to understand that the solution to his problems lies within him, he is obliged to transfer to the Prince those thaumaturgical powers that he is seeking out of necessity.

I therefore note two important facts: one is that people make their own Prince, and this is alienation; and the second is that people *sell* themselves to the Prince in order to have salvation, and this is servitude.
In conclusion, are all individuals alienated and slaves on account of a mistaken evaluation?
R. What do you mean by 'Prince'?

---

[1] To go deeper into these operative steps, see 'Transcending the mind' in *Beyond the illusion of the ego*, and 'Separation' and '*Ākāśa* and meditation' in *Beyond Doubt* by Raphael. Aurea Vidyā, New York.

[2] Prince: character from Machiavelli's work 'Il Principe', standing for a shrewd statesman who, in order to achieve his own ends (from an egoic point of view), overcomes every obstacle.

+ The Prince is the politician, the messiah, the saviour, the Machiavellian demiurge, the capitalist financier, and so on.

R. The individual, so far as he is *relative* individuality, has to depend on something. He longs for his own fulfilment, but he takes the wrong road in looking for it. This is how he reaches alienation and consequent servitude. But try not to be an extremist. We have said that there are politicians and Politicians, ideologies and Ideologies.

+ Can one have a society without power, without a boss, without a Prince?

R. In the present state of affairs, this is not possible.

+ Then shall we always be subservient to the Prince? Shall we always be under the scourge of alienation and servitude?

R. As long as there is alienation, the Prince is indispensable. Anarchy is utopian.

+ And since the Prince has no interest in curing the alienation, it will quietly continue.
  Is resignation the only way?

R. Far from it. The individual has just one master-road: to re-orientate himself towards the Pole Star, merge with Being, and re-discover himself as Prince of himself. The true revolutionary is the man who effects this re-orientation.

+ At the social level, do you think that one Prince is worth the same as another?

R. Certainly not. There are princes and Princes. I repeat that there is no need to be extremist about certain matters. There are hundreds of politicians all over the world who work for the well-being of society.

+ So do the people fashion the Prince in their own image, or does the Prince fashion the people?

R. There is a reciprocal interrelationship. It can come about that the people fashion the image of their prince. Then the Prince – gradually, innocently, gently (at times abruptly, too) – fashions the people to his likeness.

+ And the people follow blindly?

R. In general, the people follow. They can't do otherwise.

+ But there are revolutions, too.

R. Revolution doesn't imply that the people don't wish to follow. It often means that they just want to change the image, the projection of the Prince; they want to follow another one.

+ If the people are slaves, is the Prince free?

R. Prince and slave are tied to the same rope: the slavery of the world of becoming.

> 'Now have not the people always had the custom of putting a single individual at their head, in the highest position, maintaining him, and ensuring that he waxes great? 'Yes it has been their custom to do so.'

'Then it is clear,' I said, 'that whenever a tyrant is born, he arises from the root of the protector, and from nowhere else.
'It is very clear.
'Then how does the change from protector to tyrant begin?'[1]

Q. I am a scientist. I have listened to everything that has been said. The matter of projection I find convincing, but what charge can be levelled against science if its function is to ascertain the truth and get to know the mysteries of life?

R. From this angle, none; and we have the greatest respect for science. What we were speaking of earlier is something very different: the individual is accustomed to projecting onto the *image* of science the possibility of solving all the problems posed by life, even those most immediate problems arising from the socio-economic imbalance.

There is, however, another fact which we need to hold in mind, and it is this: science observes certain events, certain phenomenal occurrences, and seeks to understand the mechanisms which operate in *nature*. From the observations and from the rational recognition arising from them, it makes an explanatory judgement, a 'theory', or conceptualisation of the phenomenon. In this way are born the scientific theories and paradigms, which everyone accepts as *true*.

There are scientists – although from this perspective we should call them followers of scientism/theologians – who frequently *defend* their theories or paradigms because they view them as absolute. Now we know that, in the course of time, scientific theories have undergone modification and, on occasion, have even been replaced by other theories.

---

[1] Plato, *Politéia*, VIII, 565c-d; see also 566-569.

A hundred years ago, scientific theory held that matter was impenetrable at the level of its elementary constituents and unsplittable. It was discovered later that every chemical element is made up of atomic units which can be split and destroyed. It was once maintained that mass was the constant in a body, but it was subsequently discovered that mass varies with the velocity of the body. Even according to dialectical materialism, scientific knowledge is relative, approximate, and bound to change to its opposite. We have seen the splitting of the unsplittable atom, and the constancy of mass become inconstant and variable. And when science fails to comprehend, it becomes ambiguous: thus the electron is both a particle and a wave, two principles which should be mutually exclusive. We can conclude from this that even the current paradigms of science cannot be considered as absolute and definitive.

If science is in the hands of true researchers, true scientists, then there is nothing to fear, because their innate humility and their precise awareness will take everything back to its rightful place; everyone will act in accord with his proper duty. But let's suppose, for example, that some dogmatic and absolutist ideology gets hold of science and makes it a lowly handmaiden: then we shall find ourselves with a science which is no longer science but a by-product of this ideology. In other words, it, too, would be an ideology and no longer research into 'essential phenomena', as in fact it should be.

+ If I am not mistaken, you are saying that scientific conceptualisation (theory) can be crystallised to the detriment of research itself. Is it this conceptualisation which is deified?

R. A theory – like all the theories which reflect 'relative phenomena' – is always a conceptualisation of *something*. A concept always expresses the mental representation of some datum and serves to create relationship and expression, that is, it serves as a means of communication. Now that datum, or thing, is always related, as far as science is concerned, to some phenomenon, to the world of becoming, the world of change and movement. But we have to recognise that, at the level of movement, there cannot be universal, constant laws, and the result is that the theories themselves cannot have an absolute value.

According to Plato, knowledge of the sensory world offers no absolute certainties because in this world the data are always subject to change, so that the knowledge isn't stable, constant, or valid for everyone; true knowledge is not of the sensible but of the intelligible, and the intelligible world does not belong to sensible things, which stand for the ephemeral, but to the Soul, which is supra-sensible; and the Soul does not receive the intelligible world from outside, from the sensible world, but from within, inasmuch as it participates in the reality of *Noûs*. The empirical mind seeks the Truth: the Soul *possesses* it.

> 'Socrates: Well, now is it possible to justly call this beautiful for its own sake, if it's always slipping away, and to say first of all that it is, and then that it is such; or at the very moment when we are speaking does it necessarily and instantly become something different and slip out of our hands and cease to be what it was?
> Cratylus: It has to be so.

Socrates: And then how can something be if it is never in the same state?"[1]

Moreover, science is interested in *quantity* and not in *quality*, and the approach which it adopts towards research is completely objectivistic, in spite of the fact that Heisenberg, some time ago, enunciated the 'uncertainty principle'. Following these introductory remarks, we may say that science is *profane*; that is, it sees things from a point of view which is general and phenomenal but not absolute.

+ Does this way of acting depend on the need for security?

R. Certainly. The individual, whose nature is uncertainty and instability, thirsts for certainty, absoluteness, and security. And woe to him if he doesn't have it. In other words, individuality goes looking for its own fulfilment. The urge may be good and proper, but the direction taken is erroneous. Unless one works on the vertical line, one becomes crystallised at a purely individual level and reaches the irrational and illogical conclusion that certainty and peace of mind reside in the world of change and becoming. This is the paradox of a mind that obstinately refuses to transcend itself.

We are so firmly imprisoned in our theories/ideologies that we end up disregarding everything that is outside the scope of the ideology. The tragedy is that the ideologies/theories are often imposed by force, either psychologically or physically.

---

[1] Plato, *Cratylus*, 439d.

Einstein says, 'The closer mathematical propositions come to reality, the more uncertain they become; and the more certain they are, the further they are from reality.'

+ When we speak of the Philosophy of Being, are we at the level of conceptualisations?

R. We have to distinguish dianoetic philosophy in general from the traditional understanding of philosophy. Traditional Philosophy has nothing to do with ordinary philosophy – especially modern philosophy – which arises from an individual conceptualisation. Thus we have the philosophies of Kant, Hegel, Spinoza, Locke, and others, but the Philosophy we are speaking of has no individual human origin, because it represents that *Philosophia perennis* which receives its inspiration from the Principle itself. Understand that this is not even a subjectivist philosophy.

To be clear, we are speaking of realisative Philosophy or realisative Metaphysics, which means, among other things, that it has to be realised, directly experienced, rather than memorised. The philosophies of Plato and Plotinus, for example, are realisative.

Realisation of this Truth is not at odds with the empirical vision of form, but embraces it, while empirical philosophy excludes traditional Philosophy.

Moreover, this type of Philosophy, which is traditional, cathartic, supra-historical – call it what you will – is not a revelation or a religion established by some messiah, as these terms are generally understood.

Pythagoras, Parmenides, Plato, Plotinus, Gauḍapāda, Śaṅkara, and the Vedic *Ṛṣis*, true Masters of Knowledge, are neither messiahs nor founders of particular religions.

They have 'seen', and then they have put forward what they have 'seen'.

Plotinus says:

> 'More than once, awakening to my true being from physical sleep and becoming estranged from everything in the depths of my being, I was able to enjoy an amazing beauty which convinced me, as never before, that I belonged to a higher legacy. By realising a higher form of life and identifying myself with Divinity, and establishing myself on its foundation, I then undertook an activity which raised me above every other intelligible being.'[1]

Now this level of realisation and these expressions are identical to those of so many Souls who, from time immemorial, have had the same experience. Thus we have Truth and experiences which pertain to other dimensions, let us say dimensions that are supra-sensory, supra-individual, and supra-logical.

+ Does it, then, represent a Philosophy of life, a metaphysical Teaching which is to be lived, a way of living and being, if I may put it like this?

R. Let's say 'Yes'. Most of the time the inclination is to speak of certain things rather than live them, because it is difficult to live them.

The Philosophy of Being is both theory and practice, Truth and discipline: metaphysical Truth, because it transcends the *natura naturata*[2], and practice, because its goal

---

[1] Plotinus, *Enneads*, IV, 8, 1.

[2] *Natura Naturata - Natura Naturans*: these two terms are from Scholastic philosophy; they are also used by St. Thomas Aquinas, philosopher, mystic, and theologian. 'Natured' concerns nature which is already in manifestation (gross and subtle states); 'naturing' refers to the principial level.

is the actual realisation of this Truth. In the practice there is direct experience on the part of the embodied reflection of consciousness.

If we say that the mind can do without thinking – and this is what these Masters say – this mustn't be a merely intellectual notion for us, but a precise *recognition* of the consciousness.

+ However, the Philosophy of Being is expressed in terms of the absolute and constant. How can we relate this to what we said earlier?

R. If we speak of traditional Philosophy, or realisative Metaphysics, it is because it concerns the pure essence of things, the pure constant. We call it pure Being, because in the West this word has a definite significance. Now, the Philosophy of Being takes all the *movement* back to a central, unmoving, and constant Point, which is ultimate, absolute Reality. There cannot be a relative without an Absolute, or a movement without an unmoving point. 'Without the Permanent no temporal relationship is possible.' (Kant, Second Analogy of Experience).

If science interests itself in the relative and the moving, metaphysics interests itself in the Constant, the unmoving Point. By saying this, however, we do not mean that it leaves movement out of consideration. It is inevitable, then, that the Philosophy of Being can be expressed solely in terms of Fullness or, more precisely, in terms of Being. So we have the two points of view: sacred and profane.

+ And if tomorrow someone were to discover that Being is not the constant? That the constant is beyond Being itself?

R. We would be very happy with this discovery and would immediately seek to go beyond Being. Those who thirst for the absolute don't stop until they have found the true and unequivocal Constant. Let us bear in mind, for example, that the Philosophy of Non-Duality is placed at the summit of the pyramid of philosophical Teachings because it acknowledges the One-without-a-second as the absolute constant, both microcosmic and macrocosmic, thus transcending all possible duality or polarity. This is why we talk in metaphysical terms.

There is, however, one thing to consider: in philosophy we speak of the ultimate Principle or the first Principle, according to the point of view we adopt, and a Principle, by its very nature, always remains the same. But if we were to discover one day that our vision does not coincide with this principle, it isn't the Principle that we need to adjust or correct, but our vision.

The Principle therefore remains unchanged. Being is the ultimate reality which concurs with itself, insofar as it is essence and without a second. According to Plato, it is the One-One, or the One-Good.

+ Look, in time and space the concept of reality has been used in contradictory ways, and today what changes is real for some, while for others the real is what doesn't change. For some that which is objective and outside the thinking subject is real, while for others the real is that which is subjective, within the subject. Some words, according to who uses them, acquire different meanings. Don't you think this can be a source of confusion?

R. Today many words – such as 'reality', 'truth', 'democracy', 'freedom', and so on – are used with different meanings, even opposite meanings. This is true.

Language, unfortunately, can divide rather than unite.

For our realisative purposes it is important to understand what is meant by the use of specific words[1]. We know that, in the course of time, certain things have been viewed from different perspectives, from standpoints of consciousness that are dissimilar and sometimes contrary, but this is not important. What is important is that the difference is freely resolved. Let's also bear in mind that individuals are at different levels of 'wakefulness' and so cannot fail to speak in ways that are inherent to their levels of consciousness.

+ You say that the Philosophy of Being follows the experimental method. But how do you square this statement with the other statement you made when you said that Traditional truth is supra-individual and non-human? Isn't traditional Truth therefore *a priori*?

R. A Truth, even if it be *a priori*, is always to be experienced and *consciously* recognised as such.

The Philosophy of Being is also the direct experience of such a truth.

I can tell you, for example, that in addition to the physical body you have a body that is more 'subtle'. At the moment it may be that for you this is an *a priori* truth, while this is not so for me. However, you must make it

---

[1] See 'What we understand by reality' in *Tat Tvam Asi*, 'Real and unreal' in *The Pathway of Non-Duality,* by Raphael. Aurea Vidyā, New York.

your own, you must experience it, acknowledge it with the whole of your consciousness, and make it actual. Once you have experienced something like this, then it ceases to be *a priori* for you, too. So for those who have experienced traditional Philosophy, it is no longer *a priori*, but it is living, operative truth.

If we speak of the 'obscuring' of metaphysical Truth, it is because those who have approached it, and continue to approach it, just dabble with it instead of living it.

We have said before that traditional Philosophy is protected and perpetuated by *being lived*. There is no other way. I would say that *writing* and producing learned interpretative essays on traditional Philosophy can be not only an empty activity but even one that is counter-productive. Yet there are many who, after reaching merely an empirical, mental development, are *necessitated* simply to write, to produce discursive theses, to be reviewers and scholars, thus following the line of least resistance.

One day an exponent of the Catholic Faith told me that if, in time and space, great numbers of Christians, rather than writing volume after volume on the Love of Christ, had experienced, lived, and revealed this Love, then Christianity would have developed differently.

In truth I could only agree with him.

To conclude, if metaphysical Truth is embodied, it means that it must *descend* and actually make itself flesh[1]. If this descent doesn't take place, then individuality is not transformed. Experience, of which we have always spoken, consists in the process of descent, absorption, and assimilation by the consciousness until there is complete

---

[1] See 'Metaphysical Realisation' in *The Pathway of Non-Duality*, by Raphael. Aurea Vidyā, New York.

union with the Truth. One who is Truth has no possibility of discoursing with It, for that would be duality. Only one *who is not* speaks of what Truth *is*, not one who is. Plato speaks of an ascending process of dialectics and a descending process of dialectics.[1]

Q. Science, with its particular objective methods of investigation, is materialistic, and it will be difficult for it to share a point of view that is idealistic or spiritual or whatever we wish to call it.

R. Science consists of scientists, who, we must acknowledge, are not all materialists. In time we may have a predominance of materialists or idealists (however ambiguous this word may be), but, I repeat, this is not important. To be more precise, it is of little relevance, at the present moment, whether science is materialistic or not, or whether we claim that it is or it isn't. What is important is for science to remain science, that is, an empirical method of research into the facts and phenomena of nature, and that it doesn't change into an *ideology* with goals that are absolutist, dogmatic, and exclusivistic.

Q. I note that you do not take a stance against either politics or science, and yet a great many traditionalists launch fierce attacks upon science, and it's anathema for them even to utter this word. How is it that you don't follow this direction? I who hold myself to be a man of science, as I said earlier, was considered a heretic, an outcast, when I was in a gathering of traditionalists.

---

[1] To go deeper into this subject, see 'Dialectics as a technique for awakening' in *Initiation into the Philosophy of Plato*, by Raphael. Aurea Vidyā, New York.

R. Opposition means duality, not even polarity.

We need to agree that in the universe there is nothing to accept and nothing to reject. Anyone who opposes finds himself alone at one pole and has to defend it.

+ But does science have its own validity from the perspective of the Philosophy of Being?

R. Every human expression – political, scientific, religious, and so on – when it doesn't assume prerogatives that it doesn't have and when it remains within its proper confines, cannot but be valid. We have said, and confirmed, that there are, and have been politicians, scientists, philosophers, religious people who make a notable contribution to the material and spiritual uplift of mankind. There are also acceptable political ideologies which, had they been implemented by enlightened people, could undoubtedly have brought great benefit to the body of society.
+ Then, according to you, I am not an outcast?
[General laughter].

R. My brother, I am not here to classify, to probe, or to condemn. We are here to comprehend each other. However, if we wish to investigate reality/man, we must have a framework for it in its totality, in its physical-psycho-spiritual unity. We cannot come to a halt at a merely expressive dimension, which, after all, is the one that has least importance. The laws which govern the life of the individual and the world/nature have their origin beyond their material and contingent manifestations. To turn one's back on supra-individual realms is to deliberately limit and constrain oneself, and this is not in accord with reason.

Nature is an essential unity with a manifold manifestation, both vertically and horizontally, and science should operate not only in the empirical but in the meta-empirical as well.

Knowledge, both scientific and otherwise, must move towards liberating mankind from dread of the future, psychological fear, and separatist individualism. It must seek to re-habilitate spiritual man as a component of life and not set him against nature. It must spur him on to self-realisation by integrating all that may be known, which is the heritage of all peoples, because, higher than nations, there is a *single* humanity that is reaching out towards the same destiny.

Man must re-fashion himself on the *authority* of Truth in its totality, by eliminating the super-impositions, delusions, and idols which keep him in the limited and contingent.

We need a toleration that is born from a conscious acceptance of mutual co-existence. In accordance with his qualifications, each must pursue the duty that is proper to him.

Science can become dogmatic and sectarian 'scientism' if it becomes entrenched aprioristically in conceptions which are exclusively materialistic and unilateral. Science, in its various branches, must be a discipline which moves from the low up towards the high; or, better still, it must leave the shell, or periphery, and go to the living kernel.

Science may be of use to the masses, because it actually operates from an order of factors which is closer and more immediate to the common being. Thus, if metaphysics proceeds from the kernel or noumenon out to the circumference, science operates in the reverse direction. From this perspective there is no opposition, but integration, between the Philosophy of Being and the philosophy of becoming. We shall rather say that in the society of Being this integration is applied in an appropriate way. Let us not forget this: the Philosophy of Being is a Philosophy of synthesis, unity, and totality. In it, and by means of it, the very duality of profane and sacred disappears.

Q. What often happens to me, and perhaps to others as well, is that I confuse people who 'live' the Philosophy with those who merely speak and write about it. This is a fundamental distinction, which should be made in order to avoid falling into the trap of false evaluations which can retard growth. For years I've been struggling with so many spiritualist or esoteric people and groups without having a proper stimulus to grow. But today I recognise very clearly that many people don't do any more than intellectualise, and don't want to do more than that. I am also aware of a great gulf between an intellectual or erudite person of traditional Philosophy and a Realised or Liberated Philosopher.

R. It seems to me that our friend has spoken with great clarity, and I don't know what to add. This distinction is fundamental, and if some things in the course of time have not gone as they should have gone, let us say it again, this is because there have been more cultural *pandits* and sentimentalists than true realised philosophers. This is the state of affairs right up to the present time. On the other hand, it's easier to write or simply speak than to be. The philosophical ascent is not for all at the same time.[1]

---

[1] See '*Karma, sādhanā* and Culturalism' and 'Points of view and Erudition' in *Beyond Doubt*, by Raphael. Aurea Vidyā, New York.

This does not mean that we shouldn't read, but we need to be careful not to stop at the point where metaphysical realisation begins.

When the consciousness isn't sufficient to match the Truth that has been glimpsed, there is a total inconsistency, and if people then wish to act as masters (directly or indirectly) they become demagogues.

We should never forget that the Truth is made accessible so that it may be assimilated and lived. There is no other purpose. The 'Sermon on the Mount' or the Vedāntic 'You are That'[1] have their value according to the degree to which they are *meditated* upon, *assimilated*, and *lived*.

Q. In truth, all the sages maintain that desire is the source of conflict and suffering. On what do they base this assertion?

R. On discernment, mental discrimination, subsequent deduction, and assimilation.

Through self-observation it has been recognised that there is a definite impulse to be extrovert, to take, have, and possess for oneself. This energy/movement for acquisition quietens down when one is gratified by the desired object. However, when one desire has been exhausted, and there is relative gratification, the psyche is not absolutely at peace but moves towards acquiring and appropriating something new.

What's been discovered is that the life of individuality is a continuous and unceasing to-ing and fro-ing from

---

[1] For the understanding of this fundamental *Upaniṣadic Mahāvākya*, see Śaṅkara's *Vākyavṛtti* (The Exposition of the Sentence) and *Vivekacūḍāmaṇi* (The Great Jewel of Discrimination). Translation from the Sanskrit and commentary by Raphael. Aurea Vidyā, New York.

acquisition to gratification, and so on for ever. Here are some factors that are relevant to this point:

1. Acquisition creates resistance and therefore conflict.

2. Gratification is not constant or lasting, so that the consciousness is always in a state of uncertainty and fear. This anxious uncertainty has already cancelled the pleasant temporary gratification.

3. The actual egoic object of gratification is contingent and thus transient, which gives rise to further anxieties, struggles, and distress, in an effort to perpetuate the object of gratification.

4. In short, if the desire, or what is understood by this term, is not constant, not gratifying, and hence fails to bring peace to the heart, then one may ask whether it can be eliminated from the context of individuality. And if it is eliminated, can the being survive, or is desire such an integral component of the very life of the person that it cannot be eradicated?

The Sages withdrew into themselves to discover if it was possible to reach the state of desirelessness. They themselves paid the price, as do all who seek truly and seriously, and they discovered that not only was it possible to survive, but it was actually the end of imbalance, anxiety, and anguish. In other words, they discovered, in confirmation of the Philosophy of Being, that to live without desire is to live without resistances, to live in profound peace, to live in unity with life itself, to live without attachment. What remains is the consciousness, which reveals itself ... in self-awareness.

The Buddha, for example, sought to discover why man is full of strife. We know the conclusion that he reached after countless tests and trials. Moreover, in his wish to be empirical as well, he provided the *means* and the *methods* for overcoming the monster of desire which ensnares the children of men.

We can all verify the Buddha's experience, and, if we are qualified and truly wish to, we can all overcome desire and find peace, true peace, not that given by the sensory, acquisitive world.[1]

Q. But hadn't traditional Philosophy already provided a similar truth?

R. Yes, I understand. We have said that your approach to the topic proceeds from the low to the high, and not vice versa. However, if we bear in mind that universal truth is supra-empirical and supra-individual, we shall still proceed along our road without any danger of staying limited by empirical rationality.

In any case, it is not enough for the *Upaniṣad* to say, 'When all the desires rooted in the heart disappear, the mortal becomes immortal and attains the *Brahman*. To this end is the teaching'[2], because this truth has to be experienced, that is, it has to be lived by that reflection of consciousness which is identified with the projections.

Let us recall that the Self has nothing to experience. On the other hand, in this cycle of conversations we are seeking to present some things in a particular way, although

---

[1] See 'We are children of desire' in *At the Source of Life*, by Raphael. Aurea Vidyā, New York.

[2] *Kaṭha Upaniṣad*, II, VI, 14-15 and *Bṛhadāraṇyaka Upaniṣad*, IV, IV, 7.

some questions could be put in a different way and also receive a different kind of answer.

Q. Unfortunately, a good many so-called right-minded and well-educated people who lead humanity don't believe in certain things, don't believe that man can free himself from desire, and so they understand life in terms of struggle, power, and subjugation, even in relation to nature.

R. Yes. Unfortunately, they pay no attention to a particular type of experience and will not consider an effective and concrete experiential result. But it is also true that while they continue to interpret life in terms of struggle, dominion, and separation, refusing to consider existential realms or teachings which have their own *raison d'être*, they will be unable to solve the fundamental problems.

As long as we choose to forcibly divide society in terms of rich and poor, intelligent and stupid, middle-class and workers, dictatorship and democracy, and other types of duality, we shall fail to realise the unity of consciousness, not to mention universal unity, or even racial unity.

Nor can the problem be solved by trying to subjugate the opposing social faction. This can only result in strife, warfare, and violence, among other things. But as long as men, in facing up to their problems, express themselves by means of violence or tanks, whichever faction uses them, they will not be able to enjoy peaceful co-existence or intelligent co-operation.

Unfortunately, the tendency of the individual has always been characterised by this kind of idealism, fuelled unconsciously – sometimes consciously – by *propaganda merchants*. Until the supporters of mutually opposing tendencies give up their thirst to rule through acquisition and try to overcome their *desire* for self-assertion, there will never be peace or freedom.

This is not a contemporary struggle, but one that is everlasting, and it is here that a part can be played by the Philosophy of Being, which transcends these very dualisms, being at a higher point where human consciousness can re-discover itself in perfect equilibrium and stability.

It's also a question of acknowledging, in all humility, that there is good in some Eastern and some Western ideologies. It's important to be able to find the right point of synthesis: some communities have come close to finding it, and they can serve as examples.

People should develop a kind of awareness which is not one of competition, revenge, opposition, envy, and intolerance. They should develop an awareness of sharing, of proper physical and psychological relationship; and, most importantly, they should embrace the fact that humanity is *one* and *one alone*, and that it has the same existential problems and the same goal. This is a perspective which clearly involves a change of vision and consciousness. But, my dear friends, until we change ourselves we shall not be able to have a better society. It is a delusion to think otherwise.

Here the actions and the examples of the great Sages and their followers can be introduced to make a valid contribution at the social level, too.

If those energies which are currently focused on spreading violence, confrontation, and a war of destruction on the 'enemy' were focused on this kind of revolution of consciousness, we would certainly have positive and definite results.

If, instead of *projecting* the revolution, we were to have a revolution within ourselves, external affairs would have no choice but to change.

We have to think that the being has within it the instinct for freedom and thought, and we cannot subjugate the being or take it prisoner.

We cannot make millions of people live in captivity on the pretext of giving them a just political ideology. Instead, we need to make them feel, principally and first of all, that they are thinking individuals, self-aware and conscious of their choices, and, if they should so desire, we should give them the opportunity of approaching the divine and the transcendent. Take note: we are not speaking of a 'feeling' of brotherhood, but of a 'transformation' of consciousness.[1]

Q. I am an educated man, and for years I have been a staunch advocate of what is defined as 'progress'. But today – and it's not a question of expounding the whole course of my crisis – I find myself in a different position. This material and technical progress is causing us to lose values which are not only spiritual, as I am beginning to discover, but even human: the actual human values which this progress seems to be intentionally working to cultivate. I would have much more to say with regard to this apparent advance of progress, but I would rather hear what you might say in reply, if you would be so kind.

R. First of all, I should like to express one of your sentences with greater precision: it isn't that *it is causing us* to lose certain values – *it has already done* so.

---

[1] See 'Transformation of Consciousness and Techniques' in *Beyond Doubt*, by Raphael, op. cit.

Look, on another occasion we emphasised the fact that being, in its totality, is spirit, soul, and body, to use the classical terminology. Now the modern world has put the emphasis *exclusively* on body, both microcosmic and macrocosmic, as a result of which there is an identification of oneself with the extreme periphery of life.

What people call progress is nothing but a mere multiplication of consumer goods and items of material equipment designed to provide comfort solely for the 'body' of the individual. However, we should examine whether this thrust towards comfort has achieved the desired end or not, but that is another question. In any case, one thing is certain: current progress does not bring freedom, but servitude and alienation.

Sooner or later, progress thus conceived – that is, progress at one level only – can have three possible outcomes: devastation at the level of nature, catastrophe caused by man himself, or – and this would seem to be the best we can hope for – we will reach an intellectual, moral, and educational level that is coarse enough to make the consciousness rebel and start the return journey. When the very depths of an occurrence are reached, something has to happen. We would say that this is an incontrovertible fact. Many civilisations have been born, have developed, and, in degenerating, have disappeared.

Q. But doesn't going the other way likewise involve unilateral direction?

R. Of course. It is right to emphasise that the Philosophy of Being is not for extremism of any kind.

At the manifest level, Harmony is not realising *extremes*, and consequently there is no wish to declare a shutdown on all production of material goods. The body requires food and other necessities which are vital to its particular constitution. Moreover, in its application to contingency, the Philosophy of Being supports the social orders, each of which performs productive activities in accordance with its own specific nature.

In the society of Being no one is unemployed; idleness does not lead to Being.

THE SOCIAL ORDERS

Q. At this point I would like to ask you about the meaning of the so-called castes in the traditional Eastern Teaching. What relevance can they have to our way of living?

R. It would be better to call them 'social orders', because this term has a closer correspondence to their function. They are relevant not only to the East but to the West as well.
 The orders, together with other forms and goals, exist even today, because they are essential to society. We have the order of doctors, lawyers, entrepreneurs, craftsmen, and farmers. We have the priestly order, the legislative order, and so on. These things are obvious. We refer to the *aptitudes* and the specific energy qualifications which the individual evinces. We can also speak of vocations.
 The fact that these orders, past or present, have not held to some of their principles, that they have not fulfilled their specific *dharma* (duty) or *éthos*, that one of them has tried, and is still trying, to dominate the others and gain absolute and unilateral leadership, does not detract from the principle of the 'social orders' as such. This has been a problem, and it remains a problem today. In other periods there have been specific relationships between the priestly order and the legislative order, between the *third* order and the *fourth* order, but these endure even today. We could have disharmony between the legislative and

executive orders, but this comes back to the matter of the right balance of energy between individuals.

The Philosophy of Being offers its own particular ordering of society, based, in fact, on the different 'social orders' and their closest co-operation for the welfare of the 'social body'. The fundamental standpoint of traditional Philosophy is that all the orders, all human activities, *are not ends in themselves*, but means of attaining emancipation, deliverance from desire and from individuality as such. In other words, they are means of transcending the empirical ego. Hence the ceremonies of affiliation to the various orders. Hence, too, the distinction between the Philosophy of Being and the philosophy of becoming: according to the latter, the social orders represent channels for enlarging the empirical ego; they are ends in themselves; their aim is to acquire wealth; at best, they are instruments of power.

Q. But there have been orders that have been totally excluded from the social context: for example, the outcastes.

R. In every age there have been degeneration and usurpation of power. On the other hand, in some parts of the world today we can see the reverse process, where the spiritual order is excluded and considered an outcast. However, we must not confuse human deviation from a principle with the principle itself.

Genuine philosophers have *transcended* all the social orders, which, we should be clear about, operate in the world of becoming. In past ages the Realised Man, as far as concerns India, would set aside his *Brāhmana's* thread, as a sign that he had transcended his social status.

The words of the *Bhagavadgītā* are clear: 'All those who find shelter in Me, O *Pārtha*, whatever their origin: *Vaiśya*, woman, and even *śūdra*, all attain the supreme goal.' And again: 'The [true] sages are the ones who look with the same eye upon a *Brāhmaṇa* – crowned with wisdom and humility – a cow, an elephant, a dog, and a *śvapāka* [eater of dog meat].'[1] These *ślokas* could not be clearer.

From an esoteric perspective, then, we can say that the social orders represent 'conscious positions of consciousness' inherent in all living beings in every mode of universal life. This implies that the institution of the social orders should not be appreciated by the letter but by the spirit.

In his ideal 'Politéia', Plato conceives the state as an enlarged Soul; and just as the Soul of a being is expressed in three aspects – rational, spirited/passionate, and appetitive/instinctive – so the State, which is the totality of many individuals, expresses itself in a threefold form by means of its social orders.

Every being 'makes its appearance' with particular potentialities, the result of the combination of the three *guṇas*, which are indeed expressed through rationality, passion, and instinct, and which are inherent in its state of consciousness, its particular nature, and not inherited from the environment or parents. We would say that they are the effect of its evolutionary level, if we are allowed to use such an expression.

There have been *Kṣatriyas* – or 'guardians', as Plato calls them – who, while being such, have had aptitudes

---

[1] *Bhagavadgītā* IX, 32; V, 18. Translation from the Sanskrit and commentary by Raphael. Aurea Vidyā, New York.

better suited to teaching than to the art of commanding, great enough to be Masters of *Brāhmaṇas*. For example, Sākyamuni (Buddha) and Jesus belonged to the *Kṣatriya* order. Jesus, in fact, was descended from the royal tribe of Judah and not from the priestly tribe of Levi. Plato says:

> 'Through general affinity of origin they should beget sons similar to themselves; but it is possible for a silver scion to be born from gold, and a gold scion to be born from silver, and this reciprocity can occur with other births. For this reason, the godhead ordains first – and this applies in particular to the rulers – that they should nurture their children well and guard them carefully by observing attentively which of these metals is mingled with their souls; and if a son [of the rulers] has bronze or iron within him at birth they must not take pity on him, but they must show due regard to nature and set him among the craftsmen or farmers; and conversely if among the latter there are born sons who have gold or silver within them, they must pay them due honour and raise the first [gold] to the duties of guarding, and the second to the duties of defending.'[1]

In relation to these natural and individual qualifications and predispositions (in Plato's terms, the mingling of gold, silver, and so on, which correspond to the *guṇas* of the Hindu tradition), there prevailed in the course of time the concept of family inheritability, inasmuch as there is always a certain affinity between father and son, although it is not to be taken as absolute. This is how, in ancient times, the word '*Brāhmaṇa*' acquired the connotation of a 'knower of *Brahman*' or 'knower of Truth'. It was not a loanword

---

[1] Plato, *Politéia*, III, 415a-c.

from family inheritability (see *Śatapatha Brāhmaṇa*, XII. 6.1. 41; *Chāndogya Upaniṣad*, IV.4).

In the *Sutta Nipāta* of the *Buddhist Canon*, when Sabhiyo asks what is meant by '*Brāhmaṇa*', the Awakened One replies, 'He who has overcome evil, O Sabhiyo; he who is spotless; he whose mind is at peace and whose consciousness is steady; he who has escaped from *saṁsāra* and is perfectly fulfilled: such a one is called '*Brāhmaṇa*' (III. VII. 518-519).

+ Then why do many spiritualists, esoterics, initiates, and so on, think of themselves as an *élite* and assume a separatist attitude? Why do they think they are predestined? Why, on the one hand, do they preach that Realisation is not the result of privilege and power, and, on the other hand, are seeking privileges and dominion over others? Why, in the past, has the priestly caste, Western and Eastern, aimed at procuring for themselves prerogatives and authority, while leaving thousands of people in material and spiritual need? You're surely not going to say that today's mess has to be laid at the doors of the *śūdras* and outcastes, who have always been excluded from all such privileges.

In brief, who has brought about this *kali yuga*, or iron age, which finds expression in terms of materialism, confusion, disarray, and so forth?

There is another question related to this: why use an esoteric language that is different from current usage?

R. There is an aphorism from the 'Way of Fire' which says, 'There is only one aristocracy, that of the Heart; only one democracy, that of Accord; only one new order, that of Sharing; only one civilisation, that which can reveal the Beauty of Synthesis.'

We should speak not so much of an *élite*, in the worldly sense, as of qualified people, but this is relevant to all the social orders. It is well-known that to be a physicist specific qualifications are required, without which one can do anything except be a physicist.

We repeat that these orders mirror the various *aptitudes* of individuals and therefore the various social *departments*. There are four channels of energy which, when co-ordinated and integrated, take human 'history' forward in harmony and turn the 'wheel of becoming'.

It also needs to be remembered that they all originate from *Brahmā*, from Being, and so we need to acknowledge that they have *a single matrix and are children of the same Father.*

> 'This is what we shall tell them: All of you who are citizens of the state are brothers, but, while the godhead was fashioning you, with those who have the ability to govern, it mingled gold at the time of generation, and this is why their value is highest; with the auxiliaries it mingled silver; with the farmers and the craftsmen it mingled iron and bronze.'[1]

The consequences of acknowledging this are obvious: there are no independent classes or orders, and no higher or lower orders set in concrete; there are orders which reveal particular conscious and psychological aptitudes. Among the four orders, with their possible subdivisions, there must be co-operation and participation rather than strife and domineering. Unfortunately, in time and space,

---

[1] Plato, *Politéia*, III, 415a.

rather than co-operation and participation we have seen conflict and strife, with no holds barred. One order has crushed another and has arrogated to itself absolutist privileges by subjugating the other orders. This is how class warfare has come about, in an attempt to gain *power* and hence *prerogative*. This warfare still persists, East, West, North, and South, with alternate outcomes, and it can be resolved only by reorienting the individual energies, that is, by revolutionising one's vision and one's consciousness.

I would like to emphasise that humanity is made up of individuals who belong to the same species, have the same nature and the same needs, and pursue the same goal. The struggles and wars which have followed one after another, and continue to do so, are fratricidal wars. Fathers and mothers kill their children, and children kill their parents.

There are so many means of claiming the rights relating to a specific social order. But violence is not a human means: it is merely an animal reaction which does not lead to an effective solution of the problem.

> 'We should do what the Country or City State commands, or else persuade it where justice lies, but the use of violence is never something holy.'[1]

Q. Does the *Kṣatriya*, Plato's guardian, or temporal power symbolise action?

R. Yes. The *Kṣatriya*, or guardian, embodies action which is necessarily in harmony with the universal Principle or *Dharma*, and definitely not with individual personal interest.

---

[1] Plato, *Crito*, 51b.

It is principally from the *Bhagavadgītā* that the teaching is imparted to the *Kṣatriya*, while to the *Brāhmaṇa* it is given from the *Upaniṣads*. The universal emblems of the two functions are Agni (priestly order) and Indra (royal or temporal order).

+ I have always thought, considering what the *Śruti* states, that the a-temporal priestly order must be superior to that which is temporal. If the priestly order embodies the metaphysical Principle, then the physical order, it seems to me, must have an origin through participation.

R. The history of mankind is interwoven with expressions of superiority and inferiority, the elected and the neglected, the greater and the smaller, the large and the insignificant, but no one should find himself in captivity or be the 'vassal' of someone else.

In the society of Being there is no place for the cult of individuality or for slavery of any kind; in it everyone will be in his *rightful place*, in conformity with his natural vocation or qualifications.

If the a-temporal order represents the metaphysical Principle, this does not depend on being higher or lower than others, but it is because it possesses that function and those qualifications which are proper to it.

Q. But can it not be the case that the political regime subsumes the spiritual order? This has happened on occasions.

R. The same individual cannot be simultaneously still and in action. He cannot be in time and outside time, and, again, he cannot contemplate and act simultaneously.

Wherever one aspect has occurred, it has happened at the expense of the other one.

> 'Your words make me think that, first of all, each of us is born completely different by nature from anyone else, with a different disposition, one for a given task, another for anther. Don't you think so? ... Again: "will someone work better when he practises many arts or when he practises a single art by himself?" "When he practises a single one by himself," he replied. "So individual things have greater and better outcomes and are performed more easily when a single person does just one of them, according to his own natural disposition and at the appropriate time, without having to consider other things." ... "It is clear that the same subject, in the same relationship and with respect to the same object, will not be able to do or suffer opposite things simultaneously." '[1]

+ From the empirical or sensory point of view, how is it possible not to interpret everything in hierarchical terms of higher and lower, and so on?

R. That's right, but from the viewpoint of the Principle or universal synthesis – and this is what counts for us – life is interpreted in terms of Harmony.[2] The animal kingdom itself, seen from the universal perspective, is not lower than the other kingdoms: it represents one of the countless modes of life, and it conforms to its own specific nature.

---

[1] Plato, *Politéia*, II, 370a-c; IV, 436b.

[2] To go deeper into this vision, see 'Vibrating life' in *Beyond Doubt* and 'All-pervasive Fire' in *The Threefold Pathway of Fire*, by Raphael. Aurea Vidyā, New York.

True and exclusive sovereignty is the concern of the Principle, from which all things emanate or, more accurately, find expression, and to which they return. The priestly order represents merely a 'bridge' which joins the universal to the particular, and vice versa, and although it has its precise function, one of its qualifications is actually humility, which arises from the acknowledgement of being simply a channel, a means, and not an end.

+ Forgive me for pressing this point, but whose concern is power at the temporal or sensible level?

R. It is the concern of the one who embodies the supra-sensible, the supra-individual; it is the concern of the one who, through his specific function, while being in the world is not of the world. In the realm of the sensible it is a function that is exercised rather than power. We have said that power, as such, belongs to the mighty *Brahmā* or the universal demiurge. Even the supra-sensible Powers fulfil specific functions.

According to the Philosophy of Being, the temporal order does not represent *absolute* power (absolute monarchy or dictatorial republic); it not only receives its *mandate* from the intelligible aspect, but it also has to carry out universal will. And from other perspectives this concept is also applicable to the priestly order.

On the harmony of the two orders (Heaven/earth, Macrocosm/microcosm) depend prosperity and *order* (*rta*) in the social context. These, in their entirety, constitute the reality of total being.

If the political order becomes estranged from the spiritual Principle, it cannot help becoming lost in individual relativism, in acting for the sake of acting, in seeking mastery and power as ends in themselves, and in the cult of individuality; at worst, in oppression and individual or group absolutism. Man's domination over man comes about because the ego thinks of itself as absolute, but this is not the view of the Philosophy of Being.

If the political order is missing, the spiritual order remains isolated, with no possibility of carrying out its mandate, apart from the fact that the individuals fall into chaos and anarchy. In other words, if the spiritual Principle is missing, there is blindness; and if the political order is missing, people become lame.

In the age when men 'walked with the gods' certain things would have had no meaning, but the man of the iron age, who is not in a position to govern himself, needs an intermediary, or Logos, to act as a bridge between what has been lost (Unity) and what remains (multiplicity pure and simple); or, to use modern terms, between the spirit, which has been veiled, and matter, which has been laid upon the altars.

Q. Many Princes belonging to the spiritual realm – I set aside the profane ones – have embodied the law of absolutist power, oppression, and privilege, rather than universal will, and history is there to prove it. How can the 'professionists of the sacred' be neutralised? One thing is certain: many spiritual people today have woken up, if not to the supreme Truth, at least to the recognition that there are Princes of power and demagogy even in the realm of the sacred, and I am not referring only to the exoteric order.

I agree that in this dark age we need a *nursemaid*, both political and religious, but I also agree with many others and with the historical moment in having a foreboding that a band of thoroughly indoctrinated hypocrites, exoteric and otherwise, is waiting for the right moment to imprison once again those who are off their guard and weak. What can you tell me about all this?

R. That I admire your courage and your steadfastness. But allow me to ask you not to strain or generalise the state of affairs. What you say seems particularly just with regard to those, and there are many, who have given even their lives rather than be manipulated by a Prince, be he political, religious, or whatever.

If certain things happen, it is because those qualifications are missing which we have often spoken of. When we speak of qualifications, we are not referring to indoctrination, the ability to manipulate words or pen, or such-like things. It would be up to a group of truly 'awakened' people to form the basis of possible influences.

> 'So let this necessity of governing the State fall to the accomplished philosophers ... The State, as described, was, is, and will be whenever this Muse of philosophy rules the city.'[1]

Q. If I look back over the history of religion, I have to acknowledge that whenever power has been glorified, it is because of a lack of love. On the other hand, the traditionalistic hypocrites have always banned the word 'love' from their vocabulary, scorning it as sentiment.
R. Forgive me for interrupting you, but what do you understand by 'love'?

---

[1] Plato, *Politéia*, VI, 499b-d.

\+ My understanding of love is comprehending the other, interpenetrating the other, merging with the other's joy and suffering; I mean, creating a relationship and communication with the other. At the manifest level this is absolutely necessary. I'm always reading the works, even contemporary ones, of these hypocrites, and I can clearly recognise that they are subtly trying to impose rather than teach. In fact, there are times when I catch a glimpse of a psychological attitude of imperiousness, and, besides, I never see even the slightest acknowledgement of mistakes that have made, even though quite a few have piled up. In brief, I see no sense of self-criticism. I now say: if the functions you are speaking of arise in order to 'favour' the growth of the lower, when love is lacking in those who are their interpreters, I don't see how they can recognise the real needs of a people and of possible groups that don't have sufficient stimulation.

The cynic, however many vestments he may put on, and however many faultless teachings he may propound, is someone who is looking only at himself and, being indoctrinated, he will never be able *to see* the needs of another individual.

Why do most traditionalistic scholars abhor the word 'love' but are happy to use the word 'power'?

R. Because power 'boosts' the ego and brings wealth, whereas love brings poverty and death. Love is death. But unfortunately the word is banned even by many political ideologies. For a long time now, more's the pity, individuality has cried out, 'Seek power first, and everything else will be added unto you.'

Q. One who is liberated, the Philosopher: where does he fit into the picture which you have outlined?

R. The realised Philosopher transcends all the orders of society, all opposition, and all consideration. The Accomplished One – just to give a name to certain things – has embraced the Alpha and the Omega and is in that eternal present where there is no shadow of movement or immobility, power, or bondage.[1]

Q. From what I have been able to understand, I have come to the conclusion that the democratic idea is that power starts off from below, while the concept of the Philosophy of Being is that power starts from above. Am I right?

R. According to the way you see things, which conception would be the best for human society?

+ You are embarrassing me, especially if I think about the experience I have had in the political field.

R. Let's try to examine the matter together. In a society where the individuals express basic instincts, irrational emotions/passions, as well as intellectual reason, which of these three aspects should be considered for a just government?

+ I presume it would be down to those who express themselves through reason rather than through irrational passions or, worse still, through animal instincts.

---

[1] See '*Jīvanmukta*' in *At the Source of Life*, by Raphael. Aurea Vidyā, New York.

R. So we should deduce that reason represents the most suitable faculty in the individual, the faculty which should be predominant if we don't want partisan passions to get the upper hand. Passions that are left to their own devices produce nothing but disasters. So, whatever social strata they come from, only those individuals should govern who express themselves through that faculty/reason which always corresponds to the *guṇas* (tendencies, qualifications), and not those individuals who are driven by passion, emotion, or instinct.

Now, although this faculty constitutes a particular level of consciousness, it still belongs to the order of individuality, with all the consequences which can come from that. Although individuality can be rational, it remains a part, a fraction, a portion, and so on.

If we admit that being in its totality is composed of other faculties as well – of other perceptual and cognitive possibilities which show themselves, for example, as an intuitive perception of the unity of life, of synthesis, and so on – we shall have to agree that self-government and the government of society would inevitably have to be the concern of this faculty of universal or supra-individual order, don't you think?[1]

+ In other words, you are telling me that if there are people who have transcended rational individualism and express themselves through a universal, inclusive, and impartial consciousness, therefore outside of every sectarianism based on party and class, who are beyond all individual centralisation, all emotional nepotism, and a

---

[1] For the three faculties of the Soul and their specific functions, see Plato, *Politéia*, IV, 441d-442d.

whole host of other things, then those are the people we should give power to. I think the idea is ok, but where are these men who are not men? And what results could come from putting something like this into practice?

R. You are speaking in terms of power, and I am speaking in terms of Harmony. While I comprehend you, I don't know if you understand me. So let's see if we can meet each other.

Given that to govern society people are needed who are free from passion of all kinds, we need to agree that these people – rather than 'having' power or 'desiring' power must represent functions or *bridges*, in order to link the universal Order with the human. This means that they must be able to harmonise the human with the Note of the universal and then be able to transmit the Harmony which arises from the accord between Macrocosm and microcosm.

The vision related to man is not, in this way, anthropocentric but cosmocentric. The individual is no longer the king of the universe, but a humble link in the endless chain of Life. This means, of course, that being, in the sense of *individuality*, must be cut down to size and humbled, and instead of an interest which is national, individual, partisan, or nepotist, it must support the interest which is not only general but universal, too. For example, on our planet there is not only the human kingdom: there are other kingdoms with their own lives, their own rights to exist, and their own level of consciousness. Therefore, being beyond passionate individuality, such people cannot but interpret society in terms of a *single humanity and a single planetary life*.

\+ Would we then come to the conception of a single people, a single national consciousness, and a single King?

R. We would come to find Unity in multiplicity, and multiplicity in Unity. Nowadays, unfortunately, we are mere multiplicity, mere distinction, in which everyone is for himself and strives to expand himself, even though philosophies are concocted of an apparently communitarian order.

\+ One thing is certain: this kind of society where everyone follows his own duty, where people feel part of the universal life, where one re-discovers oneself as a spiritual and material element, where power manifests merely as a channel for transmitting Harmony and universal Order, cannot be realised by the politician of the iron age. And so what should be done?

R. Even in this 'dark age' humanity is not without its better children. Even in the most tragic and desperate circumstances, the people are not abandoned.

Q. Would you mind finishing your answer to me about esoteric language?

R. Please don't ask such an obvious question. Every science has its own jargon and its own methods. Would you be able to work out the jargon of the chemist or physicist? 'For someone who is uninitiated, a single page from a journal of modern experimental physics turns out to be as mysterious as a Tibetan *maṇḍala*. Both are records of investigations into the nature of the universe.' So writes the physicist Fritjof Capra.[1]

Q. I have been able to ascertain that there is also an *élite* in the fields of literature, politics, science, the judiciary, and even in industry. These various *élites* fight tooth and nail to defend their exclusivity and their prerogatives.

R. Yes, I understand. Some words of Christ are very significant: 'Let him that is without sin cast the first stone.'

Q. Could you give us a summary with regard to the social orders?

R. First of all, everyone can express himself in accordance with his specific psychological and spiritual *aptitude* (*Freedom*). Secondly, since the social orders have originated from the same principial source, the beings which constitute part of them cannot but be considered to be brothers (*Brotherhood*). Thirdly, since at certain levels of existence there is undivided Unity, then keeping this truth in mind, we must consider ourselves to be equal in essence and different in body and mind (*Equality*). Fourthly, since the social orders are not ends in themselves, but *means* for raising the level of consciousness, then action/work comes to assume a value of sacredness, of rite, of transforming action (*redeeming Action/Work*).

Let us consider the final point. The individualities of society in the world of becoming are at the level of activity, doing, volitional activity, being always occupied. They

---

[1] F. Capra, *The Tao of Physics*.

think of everything in terms of *quantity*, productivity, and consumerism.

The objective of every activity, and therefore of every social order, must be, not the pursuit of prosperity which is *exclusively* material, consumeristic, and gratifying to the ego, but the actual transcendence of the ego as the cause of conflict. From this comes the idea of acting as a *means* of overcoming the limitations of the ego.

If the social body were to follow the four points stated above, humanity would express what might be defined as living together in harmony with the Philosophy of Being.

Q. But Śaṅkara himself declares in the *Ātmabodha*, 'It is precisely as a result of these numerous limitations (*upādhi*) that ideas such as those of social order, lineage, stages of life, and so on are superimposed on the Self, just as different tastes and colours are perceived in water.'[1]

How do we reconcile what Śaṅkara says with what has just been stated?

R. There can be no contradictions. Everything that concerns the contingent, the phenomenal, or the formal is the 'different' in comparison with the transcendent Spirit, which is beyond caste, the stages of life, and every kind of *dharma* or *éthos*. It is the unmoving Mover, the metaphysical foundation of the world of becoming.

+ Then why emphasise distinctions, the world of the sensible, names, and forms? Apart from that, isn't the hypocrite being given the possibility of making these contingencies

---

[1] See Śaṅkara, *Ātmabodha* (Self-knowledge), *śloka* 11. Translation from the Sanskrit and commentary by Raphael. Aurea Vidyā, New York.

absolute? If individuality is a phantom, a superimposition, a mirage, what sense is there in talking about castes, vocations, and *élites*? The aim of initiation and realisation is to free the being from all contingencies, all super-structures, all mental projections, not to restrain him with possibly new shackles, bonds, and conditioning pluralisms.

R. You are using my own way of speaking, if you will allow me to say so. At present, however, we are speaking of the life of *sleeping man*, of his relationship with other sleepers and with universal life. It would be good to know that vision which can help to harmonise these sleepers and bring them into accord with universal life.

Q. I think of myself as a 'revolutionary', and I have fought, and continue to fight, for two reasons: the abolition of the social classes and, as a consequence, the elimination of the exploitation of man by man. I now ask you: according to the Philosophy of Being, is the struggle I am engaged in a just one?

R. Well now, eliminating the social classes and the exploitation of man by man. We may add man's exploitation of nature, too. They are all sacrosanct truths.

We shall have to apply the Philosophy of Being to specific contingent aspects, or to particular ways of living. In either case, to have a better understanding of what we are going to say, we must start from two reference points:

> 1. At what level can the abolition of the social classes really be put into effect, if we don't wish to fall into utopia or be manipulated by the Prince?

2. What is the operative condition for putting into effect the unity of life and true equality?

Do you think that we can consider ourselves equal simply because we all dress in the same way, use the same language, have the same type of home, and call ourselves doctors, farmers, or workers? Do you believe that equality of the sexes is achieved by putting on *unisex* clothing? Do you think that by greeting each other in a *familiar way* we are really closing the gaps?

If we wish to acknowledge our unity, as equals among equals and, I would go further, as *identities* to which level of our being must we look? In a society of 'egos' is it ever going to be possible to establish freedom, fraternity, and equality? Equality means considering the other as myself, and fraternity means considering myself and the other as effects of the same Cause. But do you all believe that in a society where we have the cult of the ego, or mere body/function/gland, it is possible to establish a just relationship and harmony between individuals or egos? Do you think you can find love in egoism, and peace in war? And then again, how can there be a levelling-out of the diverse needs, desires, instinctive impulses, or those that are emotional or intellectual? In what sense can the IQs of individuals be made uniform? How can we find uniformity among the aptitudes, the expressive capacities, and the personal motivations of beings? At the level of the sensible there can be no equality. Equality certainly exists; or rather, something greater exists: the *identity of all* existing beings. Life is one, and there is one Principle, one supreme Good, one Being. However, it is certainly not at the level of 'I am I and you are you' that identity of consciousness is to be found, or even the awareness that we are all drops of the same ocean.

To come out of egoism – capitalist, individual, State, or whatever we call it – we have to come out of the world of the ego. *The exploitation of man by man will die only on the death of the monster of desire, egoism, 'you are you' and 'I am I'.*

The way of the ego is the way of injustice, intolerance, absence of freedom, absence of brotherhood, whatever the philosophy that is being followed.[1] So if we wish to establish a society in which *Liberty*, *Fraternity*, and *Equality* truly live, then we have to have a radical revolution of consciousness and first of all rectify *within ourselves* the damage which, consciously or unconsciously, we have caused; in other words, we must modify the causes, not the effects. Without this revolution, every other revolution is a false revolution. According to Plato, it is within ourselves first of all that we have to realise the 'ideal and perfect State'. Where there is no inner perfection there cannot be an outer perfection.

Man's aspiration is to recognise himself as a brother among brothers, and an equal among equals. The trinomial 'Liberty, fraternity, and equality' is inherent in the very nature of being and is engraved there. In your hearts, too, I feel it beat, command respect, and hold out expectations, and this makes me happy, because a heart which does not know how to vibrate in unison with certain fundamental truths cannot begin a dialogue with itself. One cannot embrace Being by escaping from the world of being or turning a blind eye to certain problems which are crucial

---

[1] See 'The empirical ego' in *The Threefold Pathway of Fire*, by Raphael. Aurea Vidyā, New York.

to those who are still in the world of appearances. Is there anyone who has reflected on the levels at which fraternity and equality can be realised?

Q. For me it is a foregone conclusion that at the level of differentiated consciousness there can be no equality, no fraternity, and, I add, no true love.

I had second thoughts about my political views when I saw a group of people concentrating on working a few acres of land with a spirit of sacrifice, brotherhood, unity, and love which actually made me question my somewhat war-mongering political views. They made me see with my own eyes how the individual can live on little, how can one love if one renounces the haughty and pretentious ego, how one can become part of nature and harmonise with her, and how one can even fight with all one's might against industrialism, the cause of alienation and capitalism. I mean, in this 'commune' I came face to face with the existence of liberty, fraternity, and equality, in addition to a precise intention to demolish the myth of the technological and capitalist society with a type of revolution which was new to me. I also understand that this kind of revolution is abhorred by many because, being full of hatred and revenge, it's easier for them to grab hold of a weapon.

R. Yes, I comprehend. It may be that the people you're talking about have put the Philosophy of Being into practice without realising it. However that may be, I believe there is a level of existence which can overcome every kind of injustice and social inequality, and it is of an order that is supra-individual. At this level, beings can meet together, comprehend each other, and love each other. At this level, the *object* can be acknowledged as a symbol of power.

On the other hand, our previous questioner spoke about transcending *all* the classes; this implies that no single class should assume the right to suppress the others; otherwise, what kind of transcendence would that be?

This leads us to conclude, in the light of our Philosophy, that it is only by effecting the single Principle that one can embody that unique family which has no distinctions or classes and is called *Haṁsa* by the Philosophy of Being.

> 'Slaves and masters could never become friends, nor do the unskilled and the skilled become friends when raised by public decree to the same level of honour and respect. Equality among unequals would become inequality if there were no criterion of a just limit. On account of these two factors, states throb with seditions. The old saying that equality begets concord is indeed true: it is a very just and appropriate saying. But because it is not at all clear what kind of equality can do this, we are left in great perplexity. There are two kinds of equality; they are called by the same name, but they are in fact almost the opposite of each other, and this for many reasons. One of them may be introduced by any state or legislator in the distribution of honours and appointments; this is the equality of measure, weight, and number, and this can be regulated by drawing lots in the case of the above-mentioned distributions. The other – the truer and better equality – is not so easy for everyone to see. To discern it is the province of Zeus, and it avails men but little; yet whatever it gives of itself to states and individuals is always a source of benefit. It gives more to the greater and less to the smaller. To each of the two it gives that which is its due in accordance with its natural worth, and thus it

always grants greater honours to those who are more virtuous, and to those in the contrary condition, through virtue and education, it gives what is appropriate, just as it does to the others, and in the right proportion. And in fact for us, too, politics is precisely this justice; and we must, Clinias, aim at this even now and found the state which is coming to birth with our eyes fixed on this equality. Anyone who will found another state must promulgate the laws with the same objective and not in the interests of a few tyrants, or just one, or some popular movement, but always in the interests of justice. This is what was said just now about the distribution of the equal to the unequal which looks to each, in every case, according to his nature.'[1]

Q. Many prefer to have an external revolution to one within themselves, because the latter turns out to be more difficult and frustrating for the ego. Killing or oppressing others is easy, but killing one's own inner enemies is difficult. The ego is always crafty at following the way of utilitarianism and self-assertion. I think this is the reason why that trinomial you spoke of a little while ago has always been betrayed.

R. This is also why the things that change are exclusively the structures, the governments, the names of the organisations; but it's not by simply changing our clothes that we can transform consciousness.

The perfect State is that in which oligarchic authoritarianism is abolished and the individual can live in harmony and co-operation with his fellows. This implies letting

---

[1] Plato, *Laws*, VI, 757a-d.

oneself be guided *from within* by one's own awareness, an awareness, however, which has re-awakened to the reality of the singleness of life. Only with a rule aimed at educating instinct, emotion, and thought is it possible to realise the perfect State.

According to Plato, the State is the embodiment of supreme Justice. It reflects within itself that intrinsic harmony which reigns in the universal order.

+ According to Plato, private property can be abolished. What are your thoughts on that?

R. That riches have given bliss to no one. Jesus says that it is easier for a camel to pass through the eye of a needle than for a rich man to enter the kingdom of heaven. But it would be good to point out that it is not simply by abolishing wealth by force that the individual quenches his thirst for desires.

Q. If I am not mistaken, you are maintaining that a revolution which takes place only in the socio-political realm comes to nothing, or at the most serves to change the names of the bureaucratic machinery. Is this the idea? Excuse me for asking, but I wasn't able to follow from the beginning. I was told something, but I have a particular interest in this topic.

R. A reversal of values that takes place only in the socio-political sphere serves only to transfer power from one class to another, or from one individual to another.

When the *spiritual* realms of the 'revolutionary' himself are ignored, he cannot have a 'revolutionary consciousness', but he is a mere *robot*. However, robots, whatever their inclination, have always been used to elevate the Prince and the demagogue.

Q. In what form and under what practical conditions could we come to know new aspects of Being? And on what can the society of Being possibly be based?

R. You are asking things to which it is not easy to reply in three or four minutes. I think you will agree. So we shall touch upon just a few aspects of this question.

First of all, we shall need to start from a precise point, which is this: the individual, as he appears in his constitution, either has something within him which transcends him, or else he is destined to remain unfulfilled and relative. This rational position lays upon us some clear-cut responsibilities to follow lines of enquiry and seek guidance.

In general, the East has devoted itself to unveiling the mystery of Being, going so far as to neglect the phenomenal realm. The West, by contrast, has neglected Being and has literally dived into the realm of phenomena and activity.

It will be necessary to find a meeting-point and begin a process of experimentation with regard to the psycho-somatic and spiritual structure of the individual. If science wanted to, it could re-direct a large part of its research work and discover, within man, realms which have remained unknown right up to our own times. We are confident that such work would lead to satisfying results, an additional reason being that we are nearing the end of our research into physical conditions and the physical nature of the earth. This would at last raise our sights from the totally metallised aspect, or from one set of co-ordinates to another, with all the consequences which could arise from that.

It is not a question of dwelling on this point, but the subject has an enormous bearing. We could discover, in academic terms, a dimension which we cannot even imagine. Just as the discovery of atomic energy has revolutionised life on this planet, in the same way the possible – I would say, the certain – discovery of a dimension beyond the merely material and physical would revolutionise our conception of life, our world of relationships, and even our relationship with death.

It is inevitable that this would have to change the method of inquiry, instrumentation, and administration. But when there is love for the search for truth, there shouldn't be any *a priori* obstacles.

+ I think that this kind of research would be difficult to undertake, because the evidence from certain results could rock the foundations of many conceptions: political, philosophical, sociological, and even economic ...
R. Well, let's proceed. The other question relates to the foundation of the society of Being. We shall say that the foundation is Being. According to traditional Philosophy, the individual has four motives or goals: *dharma, artha, kāma,* and *mokṣa*. We use these Sanskrit terms only because they are pregnant with expressive content.

Dharma and *mokṣa* are the two poles, the first and the last, of a being's cycle. Man is here for a well-defined duty and purpose: to discover himself, know himself, and be. If he fails to do this, he falls short of his specific *dharma* (duty, categorical imperative, which commands every being).

He may be rich, intelligent, well-known, erudite, and so on, but if during his life he has not sought to understand himself, comprehend himself, and transcend himself, he has merely squandered precious energy. 'Man, know thyself' is a precise *dharma* which has been handed down to us from time immemorial. Man, '*trascende te ipsum*' is the motto of St Augustine.

We understand *mokṣa* as self-realisation or realisation of Being.

Liberation (*mokṣa*) is liberation from metaphysical ignorance and not an escape from 'physical reality'.

So the first immediate duty is to know oneself, indeed, in order to be.

The play of *artha* (object) and *kāma* (desire) determines the just or unjust route towards *mokṣa* (freedom from ignorance).

So *artha* is the object which we employ to satisfy a desire (*kāma*). According to the direction of the desire (and hence of the concomitant object), we may or may not stay within what is just, in order to attain our life's goal.

We may picture it like this: *dharma* is the jetty from which the voyage begins; *mokṣa* is the port of final destination: *artha* and *kāma* are respectively the ship and the rudder, which indicates the route to be followed. The instructor stands for someone who, having made the crossing, knows how to direct the right boat or ship and can correct a possible deviation from the route.

For obvious reasons we cannot speak at length on this or go deeply into all the procedures involved in the game of *artha* and *kāma*. Let's simply say that people are not all at the same level of wakefulness and don't all have to satisfy the same desires. This is natural.

A society which gradually moves towards the right balance between *artha* and *kāma*, which is able to control its own expressive energy or the fuel that is going to drive its cruise ship, and which has as its goal the reality of Being: this is a society in harmony with the Principle, with 'right action' and therefore with the whole of life.

In the *Laws* Plato has as the foundation of social life the expression of the 'right measure' of *artha* and *kāma*, among rights and duties, representatives and those who are represented. The Philosophy of Being is not a utopia or a merely intellectualist philosophy, but, rather, a living and pulsating reality. The Philosophy of Being is based on the Harmony which the individual has to realise: Harmony and Accord, of course, with the Universal, the Norm, the Pole, the supreme Principle, the highest Good.

+ From what you say, I have to admit that this is opposed to the conception current in modern life, and this produces resistances in me.

R. We have already said this. Today's conception of life, characterised unilaterally by the philosophy of becoming, diverges from the conception held by the Philosophy of Being. It could not be otherwise. We find ourselves living in what is called the *kali-yuga*, the dark age or iron age, and we know that the *kali-yuga* is opposite to the *satya-yuga* or golden age. Since this is how things are, you will be able to realise why philosophy has degenerated into mental sophistry and the history of science, science into technical, materialistic scientism, religion into mere psychological comfort, art into personal exhibitionism.

From this you will also be able to realise why this is the age of Princes of every type.

\+ When you speak of a dark age, doesn't this have a position in time? If so, don't we have to wait for the golden age?

R. These ages represent level of consciousness, and as such they have no extension in time and space. Waiting and hoping merely perpetuates the conflicts of the world. In the same way, the stages of life that we spoke about earlier are also states of consciousness. A young person can directly experience the final stage, that of *mokṣa*, if his consciousness is now ready to totally renounce the world of duality.

\+ So we don't have to wait for anything? We don't have to wait for the Prince of peace and justice? Unfortunately, many spiritual people are looking at their watches and waiting for the fateful hour.

R. If man realises that all he has to do is change his mind, he will start working to finally resolve his inner incompleteness, and in this way he will not have to wait for the Prince of peace, because He is already within his heart.

Q. So you don't take a stand against the confusion that we find nowadays?

R. I cannot take a stand against anything, because whatever happens is in its rightful place, in conformity with the nature of the predisposing causes.

The dark age itself can be defined as a 'descent to the underworld', because at a given time the motivating causes were put into place.

\+ But this could have been avoided.

R. Then we would have had not to create these determining causes. Thousands and thousands of years ago it was possible to understand that we would reach this stage. Given certain causes, the effects can be deduced with mathematical precision. If we throw a rock (the cause), why should we be surprised to see it fall (the effect)?

+ And what should we do? Spend our time in inertia, waiting for things to unfold?

R. Nothing of the sort. The 'descent to the underworld'[1] is to be faced up to and not to be run away from. We need to have the courage to split open the monster's head, which is so obvious today, the cause of the deviation or fall. Inertia does not provide a solution.

---

[1] To go deeper into this topic, see 'Orphic Ascent' in *Orphism and the Initiatory Tradition*, by Raphael. Aurea Vidyā, New York.

ULTIMATE FREEDOM

Q. I can say that from the time I was a very young boy I have felt an urge to reflect on the nature of freedom. Slowly this idea made some headway, and I looked for experiences in the field of religion first of all, and later in the sphere of politics. I have been able to observe that, although some people speak of freedom, in practice they're always somebody's slaves: they could be slaves of God, the Tradition, the intellect, the family, a political ideology, or a revolutionary programme, and so on. Moreover, I've been able to see how others, while professing to defend freedom, strive, unconsciously or consciously, to enslave you, subjugate you, and imprison you.

My question today is this: Is freedom a reality or is it just a projection of the ego? Bear in mind that my thirst is not for discussion or erudition, but something more: I need clarifications which will give me the possibility – in addition to the basic one of being able to accept myself – of participating in the process of life.

R. I appreciate your anxiety to search for fundamental values in your life, and I also comprehend the complexity of the problem. It would be good if we could seek the solution together, if a solution can be found at the empirical level.

You speak of freedom, but in what sense do you use this word?

Q. What relation does freedom have with free will? Or does freedom coincide with free will?

R. Here is another friend, who is putting a further question. As you can see, the subject can expand.

Q. (Previous questioner). In pondering on freedom I have been able to see that there is a socio-political freedom and a purely psychological freedom.

R. Let us say, then, that there is a political freedom which concerns social relationships, the co-existence of individuals who form a community, a society, a nation, and so on, and also a psychological freedom which concerns relationships with one's own impulses, one's own vital movements, and one's own field of emotions.
    Since I think we are more interested in this second type of freedom, let's see if we can go as far as possible into the heart of the problem.

+ Excuse me for interrupting, but couldn't we examine both kinds of freedom?
    I think that this evening we could have some glimmer of illumination which would be useful for all of us.

R. My dear friends, I foresee that we shall be touching on questions which are not strictly pertinent to our level of consciousness. However that may be, I hope we shall be able to have this glimmer of illumination. Let us approach the question with a mind free of preconceptions and sectarian positions.

Anyone who sets out to solve his own individuality is on the way to transcending all the problems inherent in the ego. Let us not forget that all of us here are aiming at this goal.

Is there anyone who, urged on by the search, has formulated a definition of socio-political freedom?

+ Political freedom is that freedom which allows the individual to freely exercise his rights and to find the means to fulfil them. I find these rights consubstantial with the nature of man.

R. Now since a community is not composed of a single individual but of many individuals, who all lawfully claim their own rights, how can the right of freedom be exercised without harming one's fellows?

+ I find it right that the freedom of one should not restrict the freedom of another.

R. Then socio-political freedom implies harmonising the exercise of freedom pertaining to each individual. Does that seem right to you?

+ Undoubtedly. This kind of freedom presupposes regulations which harmonise the free activity of the members.

R. If I am not mistaken, we have reached the point of considering, as something indispensable, a legal norm which regulates individual freedoms. In addition, another fact emerges: socio-political freedom cannot be absolute freedom but relative freedom, and it cannot be licence (to do whatever one likes is unthinkable), but simply an order and balance to ensure that the social body is not brought into disharmony.

This also implies that the community, as a social being, can be kept free, in its turn, to require the individual to fulfil his proper obligations, so that, within the socio-political realm, freedom turns out to be the harmonious and rightful balance between rights and duties. This just balance is represented by the *juridical norm* or by the laws. From this comes the 'rule of law' as presented by Plato in the *Laws*.

The juridical norm is the foundation of *rights* and *duties* applicable to the individual in relation to the community; and that community which disregards the legislative norms is moving towards licence. Rights imply *lawfulness* to do or not to do; duty, by contrast, implies enforcement to do or not to do.

+ We have to acknowledge that there are articles of legislation which demand obligations rather than lawfulness from the individuals. In fact, some of them, inspired by the Prince, don't permit any form of freedom. So in what sense can we say that the norm is the foundation of individual freedom?

R. Right. Plato, too, maintains that monarchy, or government entrusted to a single man, can degenerate into tyranny, aristocracy into oligarchy, and democracy into demagogy. And at this point we shall have to go further, because what we have said is not sufficient.

Let's go over the main points again. Freedom of the individual presupposes a regulatory norm to enable this freedom to be in harmony with the freedom of others. To be impartial, the norm must imply or consider certain factors, without which it cannot be impartial: for example, it may favour a particular group of individuals, or it may restrict certain freedoms because it is starting from sectarian, partisan, or ideological preconceptions, and so on. So should the norm, in its turn, be subject to something else in order to remain impartial? Does anyone wish to add to this?

+ I would say it should be subject to a moral code. Even in the socio-political field there should be a code of morals. Don't you think so?

R. Then we'll say it should be subject to ethical values (*éthos*). So this is the picture which emerges from what we have said:
- Freedom.
- Juridical norm.
- Ethics.

Freedom must be subject to the norm, and the norm to ethics. When these three factors are present, we have the best conditions for social relations. Freedom cannot violate the norm, and the norm cannot violate the ethical code. By reversing the sequence, we find that ethics shapes the norm to point to an impartial freedom. This implies that ethics, in its essence, has to safeguard freedom. A system of ethics which seeks arbitrarily to diminish, restrict, or coerce the individual's freedom is not fit to be called ethics.
+ According to the philosophy of becoming, ethics, like everything else, is nothing but 'variable behaviour', and so it's not given any value, or perhaps it has a very slim

margin of application. For the philosophy of becoming, ethics is a matter of opinion, a pliable instrument in the hands of the Prince.

R. According to the philosophy of becoming, it is not only ethics that is a matter of opinion: so is freedom, too, because it represents a chance occurrence. According to the philosophy, which has no absolute or constant values, there may be freedom or there may not be freedom, because it depends on what is happening, on political circumstances, on historical *necessity*. It is in the name of this historical *necessity* that acts have been perpetrated by men as *homo besti*a rather than as *homo sapiens*. In the name of historical requirement/necessity, people have justified actions involving nuclear weapons, gas chambers, torture, and massacres of all sorts in the East and West, North and South without exception. If we speak of ethics, we are not referring to the habit, the custom, of wearing clothing with particular features, greeting others in one way or another, or things of this kind. The ethics we are speaking of is something more, and doesn't even refer to human individuality.

Let's take an example. In your view, is it ethical to assume the right, as an individual or a group, to kill other people at one's pleasure? Is it ethical to exploit the ignorant or the mentally weak? Is it ethical that one group's desire for power should disadvantage another group? Is it ethical for a few incapable people to govern the majority? Is it ethical to consider others as playthings for one's own ends? Is it ethical to kill an innocent and blameless person for ideological goals in which he can then play no part? How do you answer me?

\+ I agree. I cannot accept any of this.

R. Then we must agree that if the individual, in exercising his freedom, is subject to the norm, the law-giver is subject to ethics in formulating that norm. However, if on the one hand certain individuals or groups of individuals have typical customs in space and time, on the other hand there are ethical norms which concern, not the individual as such, but the being as a species, such as humanity. In other words, there are fundamental norms for beings that are organised into communities.

Where there are two beings, there must also necessarily be a basic way of behaving, a right way of acting, that is, a code of ethics which represents the principle and *raison d'être* of the lives of these two. Ethics, therefore is concerned with right action, correct behaviour.

\+ I admit that if, at the heart of the being, there is no system of ethics, then there cannot be osmosis between individuals, but I wonder which principles should inspire this ethical system. I think this question should also be put, underlying the one that was put earlier.

R. It had seemed to me that this would have emerged from our earlier discussion, but perhaps we haven't yet understood each other and will need to continue the discussion.

First of all, going back to this topic, I would like to remind you that we are dealing with socio-political freedom. This is one of the freedoms relating to individuals in a social body.

So what principles should inspire ethics? The questioner gives us to understand that a juridical norm must be inspired by certain principles. We thus have the situation where man's conduct, for his own harmonious co-existence, must conform to principles which apply necessarily to all (universal) and which are the foundation of social life.

Although a community may accept polygamy, divorce, abortion, the exercise of some political rights at a certain age, and so on, while other communities may not accept them, all the social groupings on this planet have to keep to common basic principles, as, for example, the consideration of life as sacred and inviolable, or the consideration that the *other*, as a living being with reactive/sensory possibilities, cannot be subjected to slavery or exploitation, and so on. Indeed we speak of the fundamental *Rights* of man, which are already ratified by different constitutions, but unfortunately not put into effect. These rights refer to man as a *species*, as a rational being, and are therefore valid all over the planet, since they are not directed at individual states as juridical Entities.

In addition, ethics must safeguard individual freedom in its fullest extent. A system of ethics which continually restricts not only the impulses of freedom but also their practical expression (means for attaining the end) is moving towards an imprisoning totalitarianism and therefore towards the end of freedom. So we shall say that the science of ethics which must inspire the norm is the one which is always a greater expression of freedom of thought, of feeling, and of conduct in the sphere of *rightful human relationships*. In conclusion, we therefore have:

- Freedom.
- Juridical norm.
- Ethical norm.
- Universal principle.

From this perspective freedom itself is subject to Principle, or, better still, to *Dharma* or the universal *éthos*, which is of a supra-individual order. In this we can recognise the state as a reflection or copy of the *universal Order*, that ideal state proposed by Plato in the *Politéia*.

Q. We know that there are legislative norms which draw their inspiration from lofty ethical systems, but unfortunately, as you say, they are not put into practice. Why?

Man's paradox is this: acknowledging his own suffering, he works, studies, and finds the very means to eliminate it; then, having discovered these means, he fails to put them into practice, choosing to continue to suffer. Revolutions take place with the potential for changing something, and after a couple of years it's discovered that, in fact, nothing has changed. The only change is that privilege has passed from one group to another, from one Prince to another. Why does this keep happening?

R. All things considered, humanity has already had so many philosophical truths, so much ethical inspiration, so many juridical norms, and so on, that it shouldn't need to worry about finding new ones. It would be sufficient to read the constitutions of some nations, to read some of the resolutions of that body which is nowadays known as the UN, to appreciate how many beautiful things we are able to write. But the problem goes deeper, because it concerns the very consciousness of the individual and his psychological constitution. Unless we change the *causes* of disharmony, we shall never be able to effect beautiful constitutions or have authentic social revolutions. The essential point is that, to be harmonious and to impart harmony, man must transform himself and effect a revolution, of course, but not an external revolution, which merely changes structures or substitutes a new Prince, but an internal revolution, which will transform his own consciousness.

If we are going to remain slaves to our passions and to individualism, shall we ever be able to have a community which is free and equable? If the being does not subject itself to Principle and merge into Being, it will continue to project the Saviour/Prince outside itself.

Q. This is the point. I have spoken of psychological freedom, because in my experience I have come to realise that, however free I may be to undertake an action at the social level, I am prevented from carrying it out by some of my own psychological conditionings. There was a time when I suffered greatly from an inferiority complex and, although no one forbade me to do certain things, I was a slave to my own condition. Sometimes it seemed to me that some of my choices were determined by unknown or unconscious factors. What's more, I agree with you: unless man changes his greed, his thirst for power and vanity, what is the use of his institutions and his juridical norms or systems of ethics? When men are sadly egoistic, separatist, and competitive, what is the use of fine laws and institutional changes? Is it likely that, by changing a democracy into a dictatorship or vice versa, they will become angels and be free from the thirst for self-assertion and greed?

R. We have spoken of a political freedom which is connected to a social fabric, a freedom which is inherent in the individual as part of a society or group, as an expression of co-existence and relations among individuals. Now the question shifts, and we have to speak of psychological freedom, of a kind of freedom in which the *other* is myself.

Freedom means absence of obstacles in the effecting of an end and the consequent possibility of co-ordinating the means of attaining this end.

We have to bear in mind, however, that political freedom, in its broad sense, and psychological freedom are relative. They are born and they live at the level of duality.

Q. Excuse me for interrupting. There are some teachings which propound an *absolute freedom* with regard to the individual. What relationship can they have with what we are saying?

R. None. Some teachings do indeed maintain that other beings *exist* and *are* insofar as 'I' merely think of them. Since others exist because 'I' alone exist, then 'I', as the true and only Prince that exists, can arrogate to myself the right to do, or not do, what I wish with the others, who are my 'subjects', my products. In short, it is a theory which is solipsistic, subjectivist, and egocentric. To speak of absolute freedom with reference to the ego is a contradiction in terms: the two terms, 'I' and 'freedom', are mutually exclusive.

+ If the others, too, have this conception, where are we going to end?

R. With the strongest winning. Hence the desire for power and the *predication* of the desire for power.

From this point of view, freedom corresponds with force, with power, and no longer with the norm and ethics or universal *Dharma*.

In other words, it is the law of the strongest.

\+ The law of the jungle?

R. To put it simply: Yes, it is this law.

Let us come back to ourselves. Psychological freedom implies two factors: a being which is seeking to locate itself in freedom and something within the being itself which is raising obstacles.

Psychological freedom consists in the realisation of that *norm* which harmonises impulses with the instrument which is equipped to materialise them.

So if we have a desire to walk, in order to freely practise this action, we must establish a just relationship between the desire/impulse and the coarse physical instrument which has to fulfil the action, and there may be physical *reactions* which impose rest, staying still. Hence psychological freedom is the result of the harmony between the will to do, or not do, and the psychosomatic forces which are needed to lead to the fulfilment of the action.

In the realm of socio-political freedom, these correspond to the executive body as a whole, which has to support the fulfilment of that goal which the individual aims to effect in the realm of social freedom.

The executive apparatus of the state is, or should be, a body of energy equipped to support the fulfilment of the exercise of individual freedom. The psychosomatic body is also a functional whole equipped to fulfil the objectives of the being. Some of the mechanism can get jammed, and this can create conflict between the being's freedom to act or not to act and its programming and objective implementation.

Q. I am of the view that the problem is much deeper and more extensive.

It's not simply a question of harmonising desires with operational means. To what extent, I wonder, am I free from desire itself? To what extent am I free from the determinations of my own unconscious and collective unconscious? When I am driven by a desire, an ideal, by subconscious contents, to what extent can I consider myself truly free? In short, what I would like to know is this: is man also free not to do, not to act, not to be under compulsion?

R. There is no doubt that the problem is more complex, but it is mainly relevant to realisative Metaphysics.

As long as we are at the level of socio-political freedom and psychological freedom, we continue to remain in the intra-individual domain and therefore at the level of necessity. Where there is an ego or several egos, there is also necessity, although one may have a greater or smaller margin of freedom. On the other hand, when we consider the question of leaving the realm of the ego and its effects, things change, and then we shall at last be able to speak of true freedom – freedom from every possible necessity; we shall be able to speak of freedom of the Being as the Principle and metaphysical Essence. We shall say that the first two freedoms are illusory freedoms, because they belong to that egoic ghost which, although it may be relatively free to do or not to do, will never be able to find its own completion, its own peace, or its own fulfilment.

There are individualities which are interested in directing the relative freedom of individual beings (and this is their *dharma*), and there are consciousnesses which are awaking to the recognition that true freedom coincides neither with the social norm nor with the individual psychological norm, but with something which transcends individuality subject to necessity.

Is there anything with which we can make the freedom of Being correspond?

+ It has often been said that true freedom is freedom from the ego, not freedom of the ego; so freedom or liberation corresponds with absence of the ego.

R. Certainly. The freedom of the ego is an illusory freedom, and although, in the world of individuals, we can think up means and philosophical and political ideologies, we cannot give freedom to the ego, because the ego is itself necessity and conflict.

There are peoples who have experienced poverty and wealth, democracy and dictatorship, ignorance and culture, but unfortunately they have neither found nor realised what is usually referred to as 'paradise' on earth.

+ True freedom lies in the absence of desire, but I think that this corresponds to what has been said.

R. Desire implies a 'moving towards'. Desire implies seeking to obtain what one doesn't have; it means being motivated by dissatisfaction. Now wherever there is dissatisfaction, there cannot be calmness and fullness. Wherever there is a tendency towards something one doesn't have, it means that one is incomplete, that one lacks something.

The world of the ego is lack, *deprivation*, and its *continuance* is guaranteed by acquisitive and compensatory desire. But desire and its gratification don't make anyone happy, because, if it were so, then most of humanity would be fulfilled, whereas this is not the case. We know that the ego, having gratified one desire, goes to another desire, being never in peace and never satisfied.

The life of the ego is an unceasing struggle to satisfy itself, expand itself, and compensate itself; and just to survive, it invents truly sublime ideals, which later are revealed as escapism.

The life of the ego is a life of objectivised aspirations, experimentations, simply because it is not and has not. Someone who truly is does not seek, does not experiment, does not aspire to anything, because, in truth, he *is*.

+ With your permission, in my latest meditations I found that freedom of Being, final and real *freedom*, corresponds with Truth. Can you confirm that for me?

R. 'And the Truth will make you free', says Jesus.

If necessity is identified with ignorance, with alienation, and with transient phenomena, it seems natural to us that freedom, in its turn, is identified with ultimate Truth or Reality as such. What is Real is True.

From this perspective we can also add that if desire corresponds with the ego or individuality, then Will corresponds with Being. Being has within it the possibility of manifesting in indefinite[1] expressions of life (and not only with regard to human life), just as it has within it

---

[1] See *Tat Tvam Asi*, page 54, Aurea Vidyā, New York: 'We need to look carefully at these two terms: "infinite" and "indefinite". "Infinite", in its purest meaning, is "beyond all limit, series, beginning, and end; beyond all conditioning, number, point, line, and constraint". The "indefinite" is a series of data which, although they may extend indefinitely, are nevertheless finite and under the law of necessity. Thus a series of numbers, which can be combined indefinitely with each other, is still finite.'

the possibility of being that which is beyond all manifestation – gross, subtle, and causal – and therefore beyond all possible necessity.[1]

True realisation consists in re-discovering the Freedom/Truth/Will which is consubstantial with Being.

---

[1] The subject of this chapter is of fundamental importance. For a deeper understanding, see Raphael, 'Freedom and Slavery' in *At the Source of Life*. Aurea Vidyā, New York.

PEACE AND CLASS CO-OPERATION

Q. We are all interested in peace and co-operation among the social classes, but unfortunately we have struggled for this principle for thousands of years without solving the problem. Why? Who will be able to give tangible salvation to humanity in its precarious position?

R. Look, peace is not a cause but an effect. There is no doubt that everyone wants peace, social justice, and order, but these things are the consequences of actions which play themselves out at particular levels of the individual himself. There is no political ideology which doesn't imagine that it will establish peace, employment, social justice, order, and so forth. However, unless one first of all finds peace in one's own heart, how will one be able to claim to establish it outside oneself? Unless one tries to live the meaning of justice within oneself, what are the prospects of being able to expect it in the social body?

The struggle of the different social orders is not resolved by trying to throw down or dishonour the opposing orders, or by establishing class dictatorships under the command of the Prince, whichever way they incline. When it reaches the point of having a fight, it means that there has been a breakdown in relationships and reasonable actions.

One cannot, in the name of social justice and freedom, use force to impose one's own philosophy of life, be it political, religious, or whatever, because this undermines that very principle of justice and freedom for which one is striving. Certain actions, unfortunately, carry within them the seed of contradiction and incoherence. In what sense can we speak of peace, order, and progress, if our own action is actually aggressive and violent? In what sense can we speak of social justice if our struggle hurts and humiliates?

Do we perhaps wish to establish peace by annihilating and destroying our enemy? If so, we are not seeking peace and justice, but we merely wish to eliminate those who act as barriers to our philosophy, our political or religious creed. In other words, we have to decide whether to seek peaceful *co-operation* or warfare among the members of the social body. For if we choose war, then every member or social order can feel justified in taking up arms in order to impose its own philosophy with the use of force and violence. But this is the code of the jungle, the code of the solipsistic Prince.

Social inequalities are not resolved by means of opposition, war, or the hope of the total elimination of one of the orders. Strife and rebellion cause division, estrangement, and disintegration, not co-operation, sharing, and unification. We cannot unify the world by knocking down our opponents and looking upon our own order as the exclusive holder of a universal mission, as the repository of world salvation. If this is how things are, then this hypothetical order is professing, without realising it, an absolutist and dogmatic religion which, in the name of a mission to accomplish, destroys heretics and 'barbarians' by means of violence and head-on clashes rather than going to meet with the sceptre of reason and dialogue.

Haven't people already employed these means to impose their own religion, their own politics, their own philosophy, and their own authority?

We believe that the human problem cannot be resolved by means of war among the different social orders, and thus among individuals, or by presenting false paradises on earth. We have often said that the solution lies not in tearing down institutions and other bodies – although, of course, this can be done in space and time – but rather, and essentially, in effecting a revolution of consciousness in order to found the 'society of Being', a society in which all the individuals, and hence all the social orders, are first of all *engaged in re-educating* their individualised energies, in their proper direction, and in their submission to the transcendent and supra-individual Principle, which is, in fact, Being; and secondly, are working *towards* the establishment of *co-operation* among the different orders, in conformity with that law of Being which acknowledges all men as children of the same essence, and all on the road towards the same goal. We have said that the four traditional orders are all born from *Brahmā*, or Being.

'His mouth became *Brāhmaṇa*; the Lawgiver/Warrior (*Kṣatriya*) was brought forth from his arms; his thighs were the Entrepreneur (*Vaiśya*); from his feet was born the Labourer (*Śūdra*)'[1] so that they represent the body of *Brahmā*, each with his specific function. Between the 'word', the 'arms', the 'legs', and the 'feet' – if a harmonious action is desired – there has to be co-operation and integration, not confusion and disharmony. This implies that, if we wish to solve the problem at its roots, we have to acknowledge that as long as we centre our way of life

---

[1] *Ṛg Veda*, X, 90.

upon the desire to possess, egoism, greed, violence, envy, revenge, and retaliation, there is no political system or philosophy, be it democratic or totalitarian, which will be able to root out the disharmony effectively. Of course, politics offers institutions and even social revolution, but it doesn't offer a revolution of consciousness because it works exclusively at a horizontal, objectivistic level and not vertically.

The salvation of the individual lies in the hands of those who have spoken, and are able to speak, not to the 'outer' image of being, but to the 'inner' image. In other words, salvation is synonymous with Realisation, and Realisation does not entail the objective structure of society, but the inner and spiritual structure proper to consciousness. The external world is nothing but the representation and reflection of our thoughts, our inclinations, and level of consciousness. From this perspective, every people has the government and the legislation that it deserves.

We can have salvation from a philosophy which knows how to put the accent on the *transformation of the consciousnesses*,[1] which can point to an ethics which is not limited to the intra-human and intra-individual, but that allows one to lift one's gaze beyond one's own contingent, *individual* and class interest.

We can have salvation from a philosophy which can illuminate each and every consciousness to the awakening of its full potential of being, guide man from the particular to the universal, and cause him to comprehend and experience the fact that true fulfilment does not reside in greed or the possession of vain things, but in the reality

---

[1] See 'Solution' in *At the Source of Life*, by Raphael. Aurea Vidyā, New York.

of his very own Being. If all the energy that is employed in schools were directed to the discovery of oneself as Being, I think that, step by step, we would have a better and more co-operative humanity. Peace, being first of all the inheritance of one's own heart, would at last be able to find an outlet in society as a natural and logical consequence.

+ Do you think that this kind of philosophy can be realised through the progress of mankind?

R. My brother, time leads into time, and progress, which is time, represents a projection of the idle mind.
   Postponing the problem of Being to a nebulous tomorrow is an excuse made by the ego, which is seeking to perpetuate itself. Tomorrow is a deception. In the world of becoming there is no solution to problems.

Q. In today's world there are two deeply opposed philosophical trends. One is the trend of materialism, which maintains that everything is matter and that spirit itself is an epiphenomenon of matter. Not believing in any God, any transcendent Being, anything in itself, or whatever, it puts its trust in the individual and hails him as the exclusive cause of the transformation of both society and nature. It is objectivistic, because it believes that reality is that which is external to sensory awareness.[1]
   The other trend is idealistic/spiritual. It maintains, by contrast, that reality is spiritual and that matter is an epiphenomenon of spirit. To put it concisely, this philosophy is the opposite of the materialist philosophy. Of course,

---

[1] See 'Sensorial Materialism', in *Beyond Doubt*, by Raphael. Aurea Vidyā, New York.

from them have come two different and opposed political stances which have given rise to a barrage of criticism, insults, and even armed confrontations.

I have pondered, I have read many books, I have approached some 'qualified' people, and I have reached the conclusion that both of these philosophies are dogmatic, absolutist, and reactionary. Moreover, the supporters of the first, in the name of material well-being, are trying to make man a mere cog in a colossal bureaucratic or industrial machine which alienates and demoralises thousands of individuals by depriving them of all powers and rights. Adherents of the second philosophy, in the name of some spiritual transcendence, 'put man to sleep' at the social level by exploiting him, impoverishing him, and debasing him as a person, while they desperately try to hang on to privileges in every sphere. History gives me confirmation of what I'm saying. Princes fight amongst themselves solely for power supremacy, not to improve the consciousness of the people, even if some improvements do occur as a natural consequence of the way things turn out.

I have had to give a picture which is very sketchy and, naturally, incomplete, as an introduction to my question, which is this: When the Philosophy of Being is transposed to the plane of human activity, what positions does it adopt? I don't know if anything has emerged from the earlier discussions, but I would like to have a clear and specific answer, if possible.

R. I think that everyone here has grasped the meaning of the question. The problems are huge and laden with consequences, and we certainly cannot examine them all thoroughly in one session. However, I would ask you to bear in mind that Realisation is beyond 'politics'. I don't believe that reality is found outside of ourselves, but within ourselves, and departing from our being means postponing the solution to the problem.

Moreover, Truth has no need of preachers or Princes, because it is its own defence and is self-evident, without any politics, without any dictator.

The Philosophy of Being is not against materialism and is not against spiritual idealism. It sees both as aspects of the total reality which is, in fact, Being. The two points of view are dialectical moments of the absolute Real. According to the Philosophy of Being, the subject and the object, the spiritual and the material, the noumenon and the phenomenon, and all possible polarities, are nothing but dialectical moments operating at levels of consciousness which are different but not opposed to each other. Spirit and matter are not an absolute duality, nor, according to the Philosophy of Being, can we theorise about an absolute, materialistic monism (everything is matter) or about an absolute, spiritual monism (everything is spirit): the one negates matter, the other negates spirit; even if in the course of time the concept of matter has undergone change or, rather, blurring. I think that our friend meant to refer to this view when he said that he finds the two philosophies absolutist and dogmatic. It is true that in the name of the one or the other there have been battles – unfortunately, not restricted to ideological battles. Revolutions, wars, and massacres have been perpetrated in the name of 'Everything is spirit' and 'Everything is matter'. And this war continues today. And the paradox is that all this is carried out in the name of that single, supreme Intelligence which permeates all that exists.

According to the Philosophy of Being, the truth isn't on the left or the right, and not even in the centre, but in the higher point into which the two phases of the dialectical process are, in fact, resolved. We'll say that the two angles at the base of the triangle are resolved in the angle above. This is why it is a philosophy of non-confrontation, of non-aggression.[1]

With the triumph of individualism, and hence of distinction and differentiation, we have lost universality, synthesis, and unity; and a humanity deprived of its Principle cannot but be lame and blind. Unless the social orders turn their gaze upwards, to the universal Principle, and humbly submit themselves to it, there can only be *adharma* in place of *Dharma*, and disorder in place of Order.

Q. So is it a question of not going to the left, or to the right, or even to the centre, but of knowing how to find a vertical line which is closer to man's total consciousness? Yet today's politics are guided by material and consumer demands.

R. Yes, I think this is clear, especially at the present time. We need to find a political philosophy which won't flatten, metallise, corporealise, and level, but will so uplift as to give back to being its universal dimension.

In the present state of affairs, generally speaking, there is no system of politics which is endeavouring to support the *total* expression of mankind. Humanity nowadays is absorbed by exclusively economic, productive, and technological factors. The individual represents merely a work-unit, a productive *res*, and his gospel is made up of graphs or indices of production.

---

[1] See also 'Philosophy of Being' in *Beyond Doubt,* by Raphael. Aurea Vidyā, New York.

On the other hand, this is not accidental, because humanity nowadays is governed – to use traditional Eastern words – by *Vaiśyas* and *Śūdras*, in their fight against each other for control of the means of production. A person's value is measured by his level of productivity: mental, emotional, and physical. But neither of these orders can conceive of the individual except as an object or means of quantifying commercial and industrial products, a unit of energy measure; and wherever this human *res* can be replaced by a machine, this is merely done, not to relieve the man of his toil, but because the machine produces more and because the unit cost of human labour is high. From this perspective, the individual is dehumanised, alienated, metallised, and levelled. When the social body has no *head* to give direction, it falls into the exhausting Labyrinth of quantity and loses sight of quality.

Q. In what sense could we transform our consciousness, and that of others, in order to resolve the ego?

R. My brother, I understand the fundamental problem. First of all, we'll say that the right place would be the school. Rather than giving a heap and a mass of notions to stimulate vanity, self-assertion and possessiveness (learning, or the accumulation of notions is possessiveness and greed, not true knowledge; learning consists in capitalising notions so that they can be sold later), the school should have the noble and most precious function of offering the pupil the opportunity to transform his own consciousness, to come to know himself, to appreciate his physical, psychological, and spiritual heritage, to control it and direct it harmoniously. In other words, in the schools the Philosophy of Being should be taught as a factor of realisation and, therefore, as *experience and way of life*.

Individuality is a centre of energy which gives and takes. If the energy is not spent in creative ways, it may explode, even violently. The school would be a forge for the transfiguration of individuality.[1]

One would have to cultivate art in its various expressions, philosophy, science, religion, and so forth, as instruments suitable for directing and employing the energy in harmonious activities. We are speaking of cultivating art and philosophy, not the *history* of art and philosophy, which is a process of accumulation. The various subjects for *research* should be used as means of uplift and transcendence.

Q. How is it possible to teach the Philosophy of Being if the intelligentsia reject Being?

R. The *intelligentsia* would have to consist of *awakened* groups.

Look, some theories maintain that man is born to fight (and there is an element of truth in this), but what happens as a result?

One fine day a group of desperate, alienated, and exploited men wake up and wage war on their oppressive bosses and win the battle. At this point the rôles are reversed: slowly and for obvious reasons, those poor, exploited people become 'bosses' in their turn – it's of no importance whether they are financiers, bureaucrats, technocrats, or whatever – and automatically become exploiters. Given time and space, the original exploiters, who

---

[1] See 'Education' in *At the Source of Life*, by Raphael. Aurea Vidyā, New York.

have become the exploited, rebel too and fight for their own enfranchisement, and so it continues. This see-saw struggle has gone on for thousands of years under different names, with different labels but the same substance. Let us recall, for instance, the struggle between the patricians and the plebs in Rome. In short, the revolutionaries of one generation are the reactionaries of the next.

Some think that by simply changing the structures we can transform an individual's mentality.

It would be useful to acknowledge that structures are merely effects, mere cogs to help the social machine move forwards. So it's not so much the effect that needs to be changed, but the *cause*, that cause which is represented by the ego or the creative individuality of conduct. We cannot transform an individual simply by changing his clothing.

If the ego remains acquisitive, even if he has structures that are ideal, he will always be acquisitive and will make adjustments so that those structures will satisfy his thirst to have. We know that countless revolutions, begun with the right motivations, have been betrayed precisely because power has been obtained.

From this we can deduce that unless we transform our consciousness, we shall never see the end of revolutions and counter-revolutions.

This game will have to stop because it is a dangerous game which satisfies only the ego's instinct for violence. We are convinced that unless, in all humility, the so-called 'Great Ones' and at least a large section of humanity acknowledge that they are to blame, there can never be a global solution. Society is the product of our thoughts, and it is only by transforming our mind that we shall be able to transform society.

Q. Many orthodox academics have an aristocratic, rather than an egalitarian, conception of the initiatory Tradition. It seems to me that the Greek Tradition itself had this view. Is there a conflict with what you are saying, or am I the one who doesn't see the problem?

R. There is no conflict. However, we prefer to speak of qualification, of a 'qualified hierarchy' rather than aristocracy. This word, unfortunately, has undergone misunderstandings and degeneration in the course of time.

So, precise qualifications are required for initiation, and true Initiates represent a well-defined community of beings with their own well-defined condition of consciousness. This implies that, in a specific time and space, not everyone is ready to realise certain matters or to undertake particular functions. But this is true of every social order.

Whatever may be said to the contrary, not everyone is qualified to be a musician or a poet, an architect, a scientist, a politician, a priest, and so on. In relation to particular possibilities of expression, selection takes place on the basis of the individual's own constitutional nature.

The four social orders, we repeat, issue forth from the same Parent, and no order is higher or lower than any other, but each is in its rightful place in conformity with the various qualitative elements which compose it.

+ And yet it strikes me that the *Brāhmaṇas* not only think themselves superior and this is true also of the West, of course – but think they are so *elevated* that they consider a *śūdra* unworthy to be in their presence. Even the shadow of a *śūdra* could defile a *Brāhmaṇa*.

R. My brother, there have been degenerations which have produced this dark age. If we wish to go back up to the top, we have to take up once more the Philosophy of Being in its essence and live it, despite the reactions of the various Princes.

Metaphysical Truth has been prostituted to inflate the ego to the point of paranoia. For a long time, unfortunately, the only devotion/worship has been offered to individuality and not to the Principle. It is not the true Sages that have had this attitude; on the contrary, they have come precisely to redress the errors of the 'profaners of the temple'. They have always severed ties with that tradition when it has turned into politics, privilege, and power-seeking.

Let us therefore follow the way of the true Sages and leave on one side the profaners of the temple, the professional preachers, the haughty Pharisees, the word-mongers, the proud fanatics, those who pile up earthly riches and hang on to privileges.

Q. It's not that I am sharing what I'm going to say, but I would like to give some support to what our friend said in his last question. There can be individuals who are so impure psychologically that they contaminate someone who is pure.

R. Do you believe that a true Knower, by being amongst those who are ignorant, can lose the Knowledge? At best, we could reverse the situation and say that the impure, by coming close to the pure, becomes pure himself.

FOLLOWING ONE'S OWN DUTY

Q. Someone has told me that by getting interested in metaphysics I am avoiding social problems and the contingencies of life.

They actually tell me that in some countries there is a ban on spiritual ethics and every kind of metaphysical expression because they are held to be unproductive distractions.

Although I have gone deeply into countless things, there are, unfortunately, certain naggings, especially in the family, which have a negative impact upon my enquiries. What can I do? How should I act? How can I face up to a situation which I find difficult?

R. No sincere and practical Seeker is ever outside society, but deeply within it. All who are urged by the requirements of knowledge, whatever their level and sphere of operation, and by an impulse to understand themselves and understand, cannot help belonging to a society which considers itself guided by the intellect and not by self-interested passions.

Every individual has his own fundamental problem. Every individual is a universe with his own 'fate' and his own duty. It would be prudent for each person to honour the *condition* of consciousness and the work of the companion to whom he is roped, because there is no doubt that all beings – and not only human beings – are companions and brothers who are guided, in the final analysis, by a single destiny. We need to consider, however, that experiences are different for everyone: what is food for one may be poison for another. Not all can be lawyers, engineers, clerks, electricians, or mechanics. In the diversity of expression we should be able to understand each other and have the maturity to be able to acknowledge and respect the research and the direction of the consciousness of others. All this, of course, within a free society, a co-existence, in which tendencies and experimentation can find sufficient and spontaneous development and manifestation.

But there is something else: do you think, for example, that a monk, a *mystes*,[1] a philosopher, and others, are fleeing from the world or that they are not productive in the sense of consumerism, and that a trade-unionist, a politician, a revolutionary, an entrepreneur, are, by contrast, active, productive, and useful to others, and that they are not running away from themselves?

Unless we wish to be sectarian and impassioned, we have to acknowledge that a politician and even a revolutionary can not only flee from the world, because they are unsuitable, but – which is worse – they can also flee from themselves. And there are great numbers who, while they seem to be taken up with social problems, professional problems, and so forth, are in truth simply running away from themselves and are just throwing themselves into activity in order to forget and to forget themselves.

Do you still think that an individual who seems dedicated to serving others is moved by disinterested love?

We don't believe we are making a mistake by saying that a solitary monk – sufficiently 'vibrating' – or a

---

[1] *mystes: mystae* or *mystai*: an initiate in a Mystery (as in the Eleusinian Mysteries). Merriam-Webster.

farmer at one with nature is more productive and more in harmony with himself and with life than a politician or a captain of industry who lives at the level of activity and does not give the impression of running away from himself. A revolutionary can also be simply an asocial and pathologically violent individual.

On the other hand, that philosophy which imposes itself by force cannot help considering its 'enemy' as useless, evasive, and worthy of being overthrown. But this constitutes its weakness and shows that it is not philosophy.

A totalitarian philosophy cannot be philosophy as we understand it.

A philosophy which does not accept free comparison, open dialogue, and quiet enquiry: in what sense and from what viewpoint can it be called philosophy?

We here are interested in realisative *Philosophy* and *Metaphysics*, not in political passions or religious fanaticism, whether traditionalist or not.

The being is body, intellect, and also spirit, noumenon, essence, pure nature or super-nature – the names have little importance.

Some ideologies interpret the being solely in terms of body, glands, molecules, and excretions. Others interpret it in terms of intellect, thought, *logos, homo sapiens*. There are yet others which interpret it in terms not only of body and soul, but also of essence, spirit, or noumenon.

It would be desirable that a serene, fruitful and above all free debate could take place among the three different expressions. We think that the highest vision is the one which considers the individual in terms of body, intellect, and spirit: this is the Philosophy of Being. This is how science, philosophy, and religion could be put at the service of man, for his glory, ennoblement, and fulfilment.

Q. To what does the being we are speaking of correspond in terms of *Vedānta*: to *saguṇa* (with attributes) or to *nirguṇa Brahman* (without attributes)?

R. There is only one Being, which is *nirguṇa*; all the other principles and names are just reflections of *nirguṇa Brahman*.[1]

Sometimes we have spoken of Non-Being to help with understanding that the *nirguṇa* can be understood intellectually in terms of negation, the negation of all possible limitation. But this is all at the level of names. What is important is to understand what specific words imply. If we take account of this fact, we transcend the different terminologies, because, believe me, Being is neither Eastern nor Western.

If we speak of *Advaita Vedānta* and *Asparśavāda*, it is because these paths are truly metaphysical, and we know that metaphysics is no one's property but is equal in all places and has no frontiers because it is universal. Traditional Metaphysics is the authentic *trunk* from which come all the different traditional *branches*. Putting oneself on a metaphysical plane therefore means synthesising and embracing all the traditional branches. We also speak frequently of Pythagoras, Parmenides, Plato, Plotinus, and Proclus, as well as Alchemy and the Qabbalistic Tradition and others, because they represent the Western Tradition.[2]

---

[1] See '*Brahman*' in *At the Source of Life*, by Raphael. Aurea Vidyā, New York.

[2] For these branches of the Tradition, see the texts on *Advaita Vedānta* and *Asparśayoga*, with translation from the Sanskrit and commentary by Raphael. See also *The Pathway of Non-Duality*, *Orphism and the Initiatory Tradition*, *Initiation into the Philosophy of Plato*, *The Threefold Pathway of Fire*, *Pathway of Fire according to the Qabbālāh*, all by Raphael. Aurea Vidyā, New York.

And I would ask you to remember that this is not syncretism or eclecticism. Plotinus says:

> 'In truth, "That which is beyond being" does not express anything limited – because it does not posit anything positively – and it does not express even a name for itself, but admits solely of a negative thesis: "It is not this"! ... Likewise, only the "non-how" could indicate its "how", since there is not even the "how" in that which does not even have the "which"; however, we men are worn out, as if through sorrows, in the uncertainty of the name we should agree to utter, and we speak of the Ineffable and we hazard names, longing to indicate it to ourselves as best we may.
> And perhaps even the name we give, the One, has no value except that of "negation" in relation to multiplicity.'[1]

This statement is of a purely metaphysical order, valid for both East and West and hence for all who follow the philosophical Ascent.

Q. I would like to ask this: My experience, my life, my urge to make relationships, my self-expression in thought and feeling, do they necessarily have to give me conflict and anguish? I mean, is it man's nature to suffer, or is suffering a result of wrong actions?

Is the Philosophy of Being against human life and experience?

R. Human life offers so many possibilities for expression, and in itself and of itself it is neither good nor bad. Every expression of life *is*, and that's enough. The nature

---

[1] Plotinus, *Enneads*, V, V, 6.

of *human* life is bi-polar: the mental/egoic order and the order of the Self.

When we express ourselves under the drive of the mental/egoic centre, we are characterised by the feeling of *I am this* in opposition to other beings, and thus we are conditioned by greed, by the feeling of exclusivity, competition, and self-assertive struggling. It is inevitable that with this way of operating there cannot but be conflict and suffering, and we can see the suffering all around us: it is impossible to ignore it. And although many extreme optimists try to minimise it, it still remains here, clear for all to see.[1]

More than anything else, our history is one of suffering, oppression, and conflict at all levels, and while we continue to express ourselves through the ego/mind, there cannot be any religion, any system of politics or ethics, or any philosophy capable of modifying this state of affairs.

The cause of conflict resides in the feeling of *I am this*, and the eradication of this feeling means the end of conflict and suffering.

Now, many philosophical theories maintain that man, as such, is the empirical ego, an independent and absolute being, and that his purpose is to develop and expand his ego. So this is a philosophy of the ego. Some people actually speak of realisation with reference to the ego; their realisation therefore consists in seeking happiness in power, fame, money, vanity, and things of this kind. But none of this has ever granted real happiness or true peace of heart. Far from it.

---

[1] See 'Sensorial life is conflict' in *Tat Tvam Asi*, by Raphael. Aurea Vidyā, New York.

Well, if we think of ourselves as the ego, with all that this implies, I can tell you that human life is suffering and pain, with slight glimmers of sentimental happiness, which is nothing but a mere, momentary, emotional uplift. On the other hand, if we consider ourselves to be the Self, then things change.

The intuitive centre of the soul is receptive to the world of principles, to the universal, to wholeness. The point/consciousness which is expressed in this centre interprets life, not in terms of 'you' and 'I', but in terms of synthesis and communion, of 'us' as atoms of the single molecule known as 'humanity'. I am speaking of communion and not of confusion.

In fact, we are speaking of 'universalised consciousness', inclusive consciousness, consciousness which no longer sees itself as a separate ego or as something opposed to the context of life. Such consciousness 'comprehends' all beings, and not only human beings, as drops of the same ocean, as parts of itself. We are still at the level of the manifest, but the best condition of human life can be experienced only when the being expresses itself as *inclusive consciousness*. This implies having transcended that feeling of 'I am this', distinct from others. It means having found one's own effective existential Centre, because the ego's centre is not a centre but a periphery.

If, then, we consider ourselves to be such – and this supra-egoic realisation is obviously a fact of experience – then I can tell you that the human mode of life becomes joyful and rich with beneficent radiance. By dying to ourselves as acquisitive egos, we are born again as the harmonious Self, as all-pervading radiant Love, as simply 'I am'.

The Philosophy of Being is for this kind of life, which is not a utopia, for many people have lived this kind of life, and many are living it today.

The first, effective, and concrete step towards realisation is precisely to overcome or break the level of the empirical ego. If realisation doesn't move in this direction, then it is not realisation, and by using it as an excuse, the ego is only looking for another route of evasion, gratification, and expansion.

When the Philosophy of Being speaks of liberation, it means liberation from the egoistic and exclusive 'I' and its imprisoning effects; traditional Philosophy implies union with one's own essential nature or, to speak in terms of the empirical ego, with one's own transcendence.[1] To consider the Philosophy of Being in any other way means distorting its *raison d'être* and degrading it to mere intellectual entertainment.

It is good to re-affirm, however, that at the existential level the Philosophy of Being conceives of the individual as Spirit, Soul, or pure Intellect, and Body, with all the implications which can follow from that.

Q. When you speak of the death of the ego, it can seem that we have to lose our identity to the point of vanishing into what the psychologists call 'the collective unconscious'. I have been told that things are not like that, but I would like to have an answer from you, if that's possible.

R. It should have become clear that there is no wish to refer to the psyche of the masses, of groups, and associations in

---

[1] See 'Metaphysical Realisation' in *The Pathway of Non-Duality*, by Raphael. Aurea Vidyā, New York.

which the very delimitations of being are missing. Just as the egoic consciousness – if it is not split – comprehends its mental, emotional, and physical energies in terms of unity, so the Self comprehends the indefinite expressions of life in terms of unity and synthesis. Even here, however, a division can be made, as has actually happened, and being is seen to be divided, changed, alienated, becoming a part that is opposed to the All.

TRANSCENDING DISCURSIVE THOUGHT

Q. Politics, as normally presented to us, is a freedom-killing bureaucratic machine, a bureaucratic religion, which fails to address man's fundamental problems, namely those urges which transcend mere material or physical existence. For some time I have managed to get away from this world of illusion which – in the name of freedom, world justice, and social progress – is trying to establish an absolute despotism over the masses, a despotism which could be economic, religious, politically ideological: it doesn't much matter what you call it.

In the past I have been accused, by my friends in the party, of dodging the real and immediate needs of society, of avoiding the duty to fight for others, and things of this kind. I would maintain, to the contrary, that they were the ones who were avoiding the deepest human problems, they were the ones who were looking at being in a rather superficial way and running away from particular existential spheres and were rejecting them in a preconceived and *a priori* manner. Slowly it dawned on me that our requirements were diverging: they were engaged in fighting against people like themselves with a force even of hatred, while I was trying to discover the human element in myself and others; their problem was exclusively social and contingent. Nowadays I am seeking truth, while they are seeking political power and looking for ways of fuelling the rise of the Prince.

I have had some precise spiritual experiences, and I cannot entertain doubts about spheres which are not normally perceived through the physical senses, so that I have to recognise this new vision, I have to comprehend myself within this unusual dimension. I have also observed that the mind can construct great prisons for itself; it can build itself up through ideological, scientific, and religious structures which have nothing to do with Reality; it can enclose itself within specific systems and magically use the skill of logic to defend them, even with force (language is a force). Now, how can we protect ourselves against mental constructs, however beautiful, well-ordered, logical and intelligent they may appear?

R. I am trying to comprehend the position of your consciousness, although I don't know you personally. However, as long as individualities exist, politics has a precise rôle to play in social life and, at certain levels, it cannot be dispensed with; so neither fight nor flight. Nevertheless, it is certain that human problems are so many and of such a nature that they cannot be resolved by a mere juridical norm, by a party organisation whose aim is to safeguard the specific elementary needs of social life, by a mere change in the structures of state or parliament, by that religion which seeks to offer only psychological comfort, or by a science which tries to penetrate the mysteries of form or offers us an imprisoning theological technicalism.

Man has so many spheres of operation, so many dimensions, and so many needs, and in accordance with his existential system of co-ordinates he needs a corresponding 'quest' and knowledge that is right and specific. Politics, religion, art, philosophy, science, and so on, are essential parts of his entire existence, and in time and space he may pass from one possibility to another, because his consciousness requires new experiences and new challenges. All these factors are means of growth, if seen in their proper perspective, but they are often considered ends in themselves, and the individual, rather than *guiding* politics, philosophy, science, and so on, allows himself to be guided by them and, at times, to be so imprisoned as to lose sight of the *acting subject*, which is his consciousness. Thus we come to the conclusion that one section of humanity's immense activity is intruding upon another or wishes downright to annihilate it.

Where there is no *freedom* of enquiry – political, religious, philosophical, or scientific – there cannot be 'research'. If life is impelled by this urge (which is a basic instinct of our species), then failure to support it results in blocking that progress and that free and wholesome development in whose very name many ideologies, including scientific ones, operate and struggle.

Therefore we must not oppose the varied manifestations of life or scoff at something which we don't understand or which doesn't play a part in our field of experimentation; but we can defend that basic urge to seek, which is an inalienable element in man's development as such. We have seen that the Philosophy of Being operates on four basic lines, with possible subdivisions, so that, in fact, everyone is given the opportunity to freely manifest his or her specific qualifications.

We now come to that part of the question which we consider most pertinent.

It requires a great deal of attention to ensure that the mind doesn't organise itself within closed conceptual systems; it frequently builds for itself fortresses which are firm and apparently impregnable, and eventually the mind becomes imprisoned in them, so that the consciousness is cut off from reality. There are people who base their position not on life as such but on systematic inferences. Although they may think they are united to Truth, they merely rotate around their conceptual, built-up nucleus without realising that they are not in the Truth but in a false system or an exclusively personal theorem.

It often happens that, if one tries to touch that edifice, make a target of it, or demolish it, the systematised mind/ego is thrown into confusion, reacts, defends its walls, and may even resort to violence. The existence of these individuals does not rest on Life as such, but on the structure which they have built with such patience and toil. This happens in all the fields of human activity, even in the scientific and religious fields: dogmatic theologies have brought about less spiritual development than they promised.

If we – and it's always good to repeat this – speak of *Vedānta*, *Asparśayoga*, *Platonism*, Traditional *Alchemy*, and so on, it is because we understand them from the philosophical, metaphysical, and, of course, *realisative* viewpoint and not from the exclusively religious or, worse still, theological/conceptual standpoint.

Metaphysics is concerned with *principles*, with essential or principial knowledge which everyone can seek and experience, but certainly not through the five senses. Hence the Philosophy of Being, which knows no frontier.

The very problem of *māyā*[1] (phenomenon) is not understood in a dogmatic sense but is seen from the standpoint of pure observation and experiential verification. If we observe psychological contents or an external datum and discover that they come and go while *we* remain, that a particular order of phenomena is born and dies and *a being of some kind* endures, none of this, we repeat, is dogmatism but simple observation, confirmation, and recognition, so that all can draw their own conclusions.

If, for example, traditional Philosophy insists on bringing the mind to silence, this is to prevent the consciousness from relying on what is *thought*, on the construct, the *representation*, rather than on itself.

The philosophical ascent consists in resolving movement/becoming and in attaining one's own motionless state, one's own axis, and one's own reality, around which phenomena appear and disappear, and around which the power of *māyā* emits that flux of formal phenomena.

We have spoken of crystallised constructs at a scientific level because even in this field there have been – and there continue to be – theoretical castles which fight to avoid being demolished. Years ago a radio programme transmitted from West Germany concerning scientific and educational topics had as its subject 'Forgers in the scientific field'. The programme dealt with frauds perpetrated by scientists to validate their theories. Unfortunately – and all too often – it's human *passions* which direct science, politics, and organised, monopolistic religion.

---

[1] For a deeper understanding of this topic, see '*Māyā*: apparent movement' in *Tat Tvam Asi*, by Raphael, and in the *Vivekacūḍāmaṇi*, 'The mystery of appearance-*māyā*'. Aurea Vidyā, New York.

Q. Thought is the source of communication, and if I inhibit it I seem to stop communicating and to be totally isolated. What state shall I be in if I stop thinking?

R. First of all, there is no question of inhibiting thought, 'killing' it, or negating it. Thought, then, can unite, but it can also divide. Or rather, by observing the history of thinking man we have to acknowledge that thought has created more divisions than connections and brotherhoods. We would say that thought, like feeling, has a dual way of working.

We also need to bear in mind that the existential *relationship* can be established at different levels, one of which is actually represented by thought. There can be communication at the instinctive level, the emotional level, the thought level, and there are other means which are better and more powerful and which the individual is just becoming aware of in our own times.

You see, we consider the animal kingdom to be limited because it expresses itself primarily through instinct; well, a supra-individual consciousness considers the kingdom of mankind to be limited because it expresses itself especially through mind/thought.

We attribute very great importance – and some people attribute even an absolute value – to the mind, while for other expressions of life the mind is an instrument that is very restricted, imperfect, and material. So we try not to make thought absolute by considering it to be the sole source of comprehension and relationship or contact.

The first thing which needs to be done, therefore, is to reduce the significance of the mind and consequently of conceptual thought. So when we try to grasp dimensions which transcend the individual mind, it is inevitable that we need to review our own position with regard to the individual and, if necessary, even abandon it.

If we wish to go to the moon, we have to leave our support/the earth, because it is no longer of any use to us.

If we wish to seek and realise the Self, which lives of its own light, we have to leave all the supports, all the reflections which are not the light. Compared to the splendour of the sun, what use to us is the feeble ray of moonlight?

I ask you not to think of yourselves in terms of instinct, feeling, or thought. Look beyond these 'effects' and discover what all the great Sages have said and experienced.

To consider oneself to be merely individuality with related problems means to be in that conceptual fortress, which is shut up and dogmatic and which we were talking about a little while ago. And if others were to force you to wish to interpret life in terms of ego and experience which is exclusively human, individualised, and egoistic, you could very well reject this one-sided philosophy. Plotinus writes:

> 'Perhaps, at this moment, the Soul is composed in such a way as to hold thinking of no account – which at other times it praised highly – since thinking, of course, implies a kind of movement; but such a Soul no longer wishes to move.'[1]

Let us close this evening by saying that if specific experiences are valid and right for some, for others, by contrast, they may be counter-productive, meaningless, and even absurd. In any case, the whole world of becoming, which appears and disappears on the horizon of the

---

[1] Plotinus, *Enneads*, VI, VII, 35.

supreme *Noûs*, is to be integrated and not rejected. In this way, all human activities – politics, culture, religion, science – are to be integrated to avoid the possibilities of dualism and misunderstanding.

PHILOSOPHY OF BEING

Q. We are speaking of Philosophy of Being, and this makes me think that we are going against the current, if we consider today's tendency of scientific, political, and religious thought, which views as real whatever becomes, all movement, and all history. In brief, according to today's philosophy, the real is precisely that *saṁsāra* which, conversely, is illusory according to the Philosophy of Being.

R. If it is possible, I should like to know what you think of all this. I assume that you have come here as a result of experiences and a particular synthesis of thought: if not, then our discussions are useless. On the other hand, it strikes me that we have already spoken of certain things.

+ Yes, you are right. I have put the question badly.
The philosophical view of today leaves me perplexed, because if I, as a being, am just history, process, and movement, appearing and disappearing, then I have to conclude that the name of my future is total annihilation.

So I'm not going towards life, but towards vacuity. If this is my destiny, I wonder what kind of incentive could arise in me to make me act, love, procreate, and go in for politics and revolution. In a nutshell, in what sense and with what motives could I shape myself, having before me the frightful prospect of annihilation?

It's no use telling me, on the one hand, to urge myself on to work, make myself useful, and fight, and offering me on the other hand the spectre of the destruction and worthlessness of my being; on the one hand, giving me the carrot to live and, on the other hand, a tomb without hope.

I have reflected on all of this, and while I can observe the world of becoming and the movement which comes and goes, I can also feel a deeper urge which refuses to consider itself as a process, contingency, and vacuity.

My concern is whether this urge corresponds to the voice of Being. I need to comprehend myself: I cannot simply lose myself in *carpe diem* or in professional, family, and political games.

R. Allow me first of all to congratulate you on your philosophical urge. I am of the opinion that in order for a true *homo sapiens* to live he requires certain principles: universal, philosophical, metaphysical or whatever you wish to call them.

What can we say about the philosophy of becoming? We have already spoken of it; however, let us take up our discussion again. Repetitions can be useful.

Above all, there are certain things we have to understand: whether the current view of life goes in this direction or that direction is of no importance. Whether this view is the result of scientific research is also of little importance. Science is concerned with particular facts and has its own method of enquiry peculiar to its own nature. That science, in its present state, does not represent all that is knowable is another fact to bear in mind. That a particular political ideology may prevail at a particular time, to the detriment of others, also has little importance; every age has its

Prince. But in every age, and in all fields, there are also *pure* seekers who love the true, the just, and the beautiful.

Returning to the philosophical conception that is prevalent today, we may say that it is not really modern: it is as old as the hills. In every respect I sympathise with what our friend has said: a philosophy which is mechanistic, historicist, and to do with becoming, cannot but lead to traumatic nothingness and nihilism. Moreover, since man lives also by ethics, no matter what may be said, if the conception of life leads to a blind alley, then his actions and his conduct will equally have no outlet, no rational motivation, and no plausible direction.

If, then, someone lives solely to eat, copulate, and grow rich, let him do so; for we think it wrong to use force, violence, or brutality to inveigh against this restricted and alienated way of living.

The philosophy of becoming is a philosophy of physical needs, but the being is more than excrement and sperm: it is also Intellect (*noûs*), and to forget this is to misunderstand its most significant and essential part.

Being is limitless and universal, and it is only by transcending its physical prison that one can re-discover oneself in total freedom and fulfilment. Every other freedom is illusory: it is false freedom.

Q. Excuse me for interrupting. The philosophical vision of becoming declares, to the contrary, that life is eternal, and that the universe is limitless.

R. It seems to me that it has not been ascertained whether the universe is finite or infinite, closed or open, and so on. In any case, we can just as well take this statement as a working hypothesis.

To say that becoming/movement/history is eternal seems to me a contradiction in terms. Is it not perhaps maintained that a star is born, grows, and explodes? Is it not perhaps maintained that our sun has six or seven thousand million years of life? Therefore this planetary becoming/movement, with all that is involved in it, has its inevitable destiny: annihilation and vacuity. The two terms 'becoming' and 'eternal' are contradictory and mutually exclusive. At most, becoming can be correlated with duration, with persistence, which is in fact limited by time. Thus we would have it that the universe is *finite* but *unlimited*, that is, it would have systems of co-ordinates which are unlimited or indefinite but not absolute.

On the other hand, we cannot theorise about the absolute nature of becoming if the subject itself has the nature of becoming. A non-being, not, in fact, having the nature of Being, cannot affirm or predicate Being.

Q. I think our friend meant that the energy of which the stars and planets are made is eternal, not planets or stars in themselves as celestial bodies or molecular structures.

R. This statement is detrimental to the philosophy of becoming because it supports the Philosophy of Being.
In brief, the wish is to maintain that the world of names and forms disappears, and only Reality remains in its pure, unqualified, and uncreated state. Well, this is the Philosophy of Being, a Philosophy, we recall, that is not created by man's mind.

From this perspective, that deeper voice or urge, to which our previous questioner was alluding, is true, because it is the voice of Being, the voice of immortal 'Energy'.

I would ask you to try to understand some terms which are not usual in our way of looking at things. On the other hand, terminology is of little importance in these discussions of ours. It's what the words imply which is important.

Q. This immortal, eternal, and uncreated Energy: is that what is called God?

R. At this stage it's irrelevant to discuss names. Whether this ultimate Reality be called God, Nature, Intelligence, *Īśvara*, Being, or energy, however unsuitable this name is, is of no importance: the important thing is that it exists. As we have seen, Plotinus states that we individuals are exhausted, as if by labour pains, by our uncertainty about what to call the Ineffable. In the *Māṇḍūkyakārikā*, too, we can read:

> 'Those who know the *prāṇa* (hyperphysical energy) call *prāṇa* reality/*Ātman*; those who know the *bhūtas* (the material elements) call reality the *bhūtas*; those who know the *guṇas* (qualities of substance) call reality the *guṇas*; ... those who know the objects of the senses consider sense-objects to be reality; ... the knowers of the subtle sphere describe reality as subtle; the knowers of the gross sphere call reality gross (material); those who worship a Person (God), in whatever form, consider reality to be the person; and those who do not believe in any form call reality the void ... the knowers of time call reality time.'[1]

---

[1] Gauḍapāda, *Māṇḍūkyakārikā*: II, 20, 23, 24. Translation from the Sanskrit and commentary by Raphael. Aurea Vidyā, New York.

These *kārikās* of Gauḍapāda, which are actually found in the *Māṇḍūkya Upaniṣad*, are very significant and illuminating.

Aristotle maintains that 'If nothing eternal existed, not even becoming could exist' (*Metaphysics*, B, IV, 999b5); and he also says, 'The Unchangeable excludes all temporal succession'. On the other hand, the principle of every action must be non-acting.

In the *Bṛhadāraṇyaka Upaniṣad* we read: 'Whatever is other than That [supreme Reality] is doomed to perish.'

According to Plato, too, the Idea is the Norm and Measure of all things. We do nothing but develop this vision, according to which the sensible must refer to this Norm and Measure. The vision which simply relies on becoming as an end in itself is not related to this Norm/Measure, but to that proposed by Gorgias and Protagoras and to the current view of knowing and living.

Q. What is the most immediate consequence arising from this view?

R. Let us begin by leaving behind the sense of *ownership*, identification, and exclusivity which we have with regard to forms. For example, let us stop thinking of ourselves as a mere contingent body/object. Let us finally surrender the sense of the ego, because it relates to something which is transient and not real/absolute. Let us correct our evaluation of things, because we know that reality – which is eternal, immortal, permanent, and complete – transcends the impermanent and is beyond becoming/process.

Let us consider things/events for what they truly are: mere *appearances* which no sooner are they born than they disappear. Let us no longer get enmeshed by tomorrow or by death itself because, if there is a Principle which is constant, then we, in the final analysis, are indeed this Principle. Let us vanquish the *cause* of conflict and pain, the cause which is represented by illusion/ignorance, which considers as real/absolute that which is not. Let us live the joy which arises from acknowledging our eternity, our completeness, and our fullness. If the ego/appropriation is the cause of incompleteness, let us dissolve the assertive ego and re-discover ourselves as Idea, or οὐσία, in freedom. Human experience itself can become a field of innocent joy.

+ In terms of ethics, practical conduct, concrete life, how is the Philosophy of Being expressed?

R. We can give the answer in a single word: *participation*. And we can have responsible participation if we change our vision of life. The four social orders participate together to the global development of consciousness.

In the society of becoming, the individual *sells himself*: he offers himself to the state, the trade-union organisation, the employer, wealth, and so on, with the aim of perfecting his product, improving his image, and decking himself with qualifications required by the 'market'. In the society of becoming, man is like a chameleon: every season he changes his clothes and features to make himself more acceptable to the purchaser. In the society of becoming, every relationship is characterised by trading, by demand, and by utility. Even love follows the same law: it represents a *do ut des* which can be evaluated in terms of profit and loss. Individuality is *valued* according to *what it has*, what it possesses.

+ If the philosophy of becoming is characterised by the ego, I wonder how this ego can have been born.

R. The ego, in itself and of itself, is not a being or an absolute reality. Rather than speaking of ego, one can speak of 'sense of ego', a 'feeling of ego'.[1]

On a number of occasions we have said that the mind/consciousness can identify itself, or unite, with its results, its effects. Well, from this identification is born the sense of appropriation, the sense of 'referring to myself', the sense of ownership, and hence the sense of 'mine' and of egotism.

If you look at a flower innocently, between you and the flower there exists only a relationship of supra-egoic *contemplation* in which specific identities disappear, but if you present yourself as ego, then between you and the flower/form there arises a relationship of precise reference, the feeling of belonging and of ownership: the flower as form is something you make yours, something you feel is yours, something you monopolise. We have the feeling of ownership with our ideas, too: the process is the same.

We need to recognise that the flower and the ideas are innocent. The world of *things* is not responsible for the 'feeling of ownership' which we develop. The error lies in our identification/appropriation with the world of things. In time the sense of the ego (*ahaṁkāra*) assumes such a consistency that it becomes an apparently real and substantial being, so substantial that it conditions the whole individual. It is obvious that we cannot eliminate the universe or things (for so many reasons, this would not be the

---

[1] See '*Ahaṁkāra*' in *Beyond Doubt*, by Raphael. Aurea Vidyā, New York.

right path), but we can find a fitting relationship between ourselves and the universe. It is helpful to repeat that the error lies not in the things but in the way we approach them, and it is only by modifying our approach that we shall modify a whole raft of false relationships.

Q. So all appropriation and possession has no place in the society of Being?

R. All 'feeling of possession', all 'love' for things/objects, whatever order and level they may belong to, is part of the society of possession, having, taking, becoming, and not part of the society of Being, which has none other than the Self as Being. Here the individual is solely for Being, not for having or doing.
 Reflect: erudition itself belongs to the society of becoming, while cathartic Knowledge is a quality substantial with Being.
 Scientific, philosophic, and literary erudition, and so on, is generally a *capital* which can even be used to exploit others, those who don't have the erudition. Many revolutions are hatched by the erudite.
 Slavery and servitude occur not only under the pressure of capital/money but also under the much more effective pressure of capital/erudition. From what we have expounded, however, we can deduce that it is not wealth which imprisons us, but our wrong attitude to it.

+ The clergy all over the world, who live on wealth and appropriation, follow the philosophy of becoming rather than that of Being. Are they in good faith or bad?

R. I would ask you to put pertinent questions. We are interested in comprehending and acknowledging the Philosophy of Being. If some who profess to follow it betray it, it is not for us to judge or condemn. We can merely observe that there are deteriorations, and deteriorations can always be rectified by 'right action'.

Q. You see, coming back to the ego, what causes fear is this annihilation of the ego, losing oneself in nameless and formless universal Energy. I think that the philosophy of becoming, of glorifying and worshipping the ego/person, appeals to the instinct to preserve the body, the form. It is inevitable for most people to think of themselves as instinct, desire, passion, and egoism, which are inherent in the form and the ego. Hence the philosophy of becoming follows the line of least resistance, while the Philosophy of Being is for the few, those who are awakening to the awareness of the deeper, transcendent essence, those who can perceive their own immortality, those who reject socio-political servitude and religious exclusivism.

R. If the ego is afraid of losing itself and being annihilated, we can fully understand this. The ego, being relative and contingent, smells the odour of death everywhere. The more identified one is with instruments that are made of 'becoming' and process, the more fear and dreadful forebodings will one experience. But, I repeat, it cannot be otherwise. Yet, during the realisation process, there are very precise experiences, for example out-of-body experiences. We are still in the intra-individual realm, but this is significant.

The experience of causal, noumenal, 'universal Consciousness' inevitably implies breaking the level of egotism, of the three-dimensional ego/individual, of the ego/name-and-form. It is for this type of experience that many are not ready: they are too identified with their individualised egoistic boundary: they are powerfully attracted by the gravitational centre of the limited; they are absorbed by the power of their egoic subconsciousness. All the Great Ones have said that unless one *dies*, one cannot be *re-born*; that unless one ceases to be an ego, one cannot realise the Self; unless one leaves egoism behind, love cannot be born. The whole *sādhanā* consists in dying to oneself every day, but in a practical way and not in words. The attachments to the phenomenal and contingent world are so numerous, and some are quite subtle and deceptive. Unless one uses the sword of discrimination, it is not easy to dislodge certain types of attachment which can appear virtuous. There are many pleasant experiences, and the ego has no wish to give them up; but it is in renunciation that the consciousness can find the opportunity of flying towards the joy of Being.[1]

Q. So the society of Being expresses itself principally through the law of participation. This implies abdicating from the ambitious ego, which thirsts for power and operates at a level of struggle, conflict, exclusivity, and alienation. Moreover, the society of Being aims at reconciling all dualities, including, I think, that between man and nature. From this perspective, one takes a stand on the vertical line, wishing to rise above the world of necessity. In 'Das Kapital' Marx says, 'But in any case it is a question of the reign of necessity [This is a reference to the reign

---

[1] For these phases of the spiritual discipline, see 'Dying to oneself' in *Beyond Doubt*; 'The disciple's qualifications' in *Tat Tvam Asi*, by Raphael, and 'Qualification of the aspirant' in the *Vivekacūḍāmaṇi*. Aurea Vidyā, New York.

of work and social urges]. Above this, there begins the development of human powers which is the true goal [of the individual], the true reign of freedom, which, however, can be born on the foundation of the reign of necessity.' (The square brackets are ours). Can this conception agree with the Philosophy of Being?

R. Perhaps many of Marx's statements should be re-visited, especially by his followers, with the result that his teaching would gain something and be less restrictive.

However that may be, what you have said about the Philosophy of Being corresponds to the truth. You have spoken of nature, and it is good to repeat that the Philosophy of Being has the highest respect for the things of the world, because these things are not here to be exploited or destroyed, but to reveal, in fact, their being and existence. In the society of becoming and profit the earth itself is violated by technological power, by over-stimulation (fertilisers), by the excessive profit that is hoped to be gained from it, and by over-working it. A clod of earth, a planet, an animal: they are not there to be exploited, bled dry, and violated. Hence come participation, accord, and harmony with the various kingdoms of nature or the different states of Being.

TRADITIONAL ART

Q. If the others agree, I should like to ask about art this evening. On this subject, if you have no objection, could I please have a simple and clarifying answer? I have read something on this matter, but I have to say that I have understood very little. Some writers, letting themselves be carried away by discursiveness and erudition, lose sight of synthesis and clarity. With your permission, I should like to say – now that I have the opportunity – that I am happy to have been present at the discussion on the social orders. I had a slightly different conception of them, particularly on certain points. To think of the social orders as a harmonious expression of living and acting in which everyone, rather than having an eye on power or his own superiority or inferiority, must be in his rightful place as a humble, functional instrument: I personally find this correct and wonderful. It is difficult to see how life functions from the standpoint of harmony, because when the individual expresses universal principles in his human dimension, he can appropriate them for himself by degrading them and subordinating them to his overbearing individuality. What I mean is that man, instead of raising himself to action which is universal, innocent, and harmonious, anthropomorphises this action and makes it conform to his measure. In this way, the heavenly Jerusalem and the earthly Jerusalem will always remain two distinct and separate entities.

I share artistic experience with a group of friends, and I should like to put my question with the intention of completing the picture that pertains to my vocation. Now, some time ago, you spoke about art and philosophy in schools. What do you understand by art? How can it be used as a means of lifting people up?

R. I was referring to the art of the Philosophy of Being, or, rather, to the Philosophy of Being when applied to the realm of art.

+ Isn't art always the same? Isn't there a single art and a single knowledge?

R. Certainly. There is a single art, and it is that which fittingly reveals the Idea by means of form/volume.

+ I don't fully understand. Could you please give a clearer explanation?

R. The art of the philosophy of becoming has as its points of reference the 'body' or the 'form', in the broadest sense, as an end in itself; and for its instrument of expression it has aesthetic *feeling*, or emotion. Thus its ultimate object is 'form' or volume, and its instrument of perception and interpretation is feeling, which means attraction/repulsion. Art has to *please* the 'egoic sensibility', so that the work of art is relative and contingent to the relativity and transitoriness of the ego. In other words, it is an art which is born from egoic emotion (from which there also comes the obsession with artistic 'personality') and which is directed to the individual's aesthetic *enjoyment*. From this point of view, it is flattened and constricted into a mere horizontal dimension, so that not only is it *transient*, but it is not even educational, because, in fact, it doesn't touch the actual essence of the being or stimulate the transcendent profundity of the person.

The Art of the Philosophy of Being has as its reference point the Idea, the Principle, the purely Beautiful, the True; as its instrument of perception it has super-conscious intuition (while the artist of the philosophy of becoming takes a great deal from the subconscious and intermediary mental sphere), and as support for its manifestation it has form or volume.

The aesthetics of the Philosophy of Being is not related to pleasure and pain, attraction and repulsion, enjoyment/pleasure or rejection, but is related to Beauty, Harmony, and accord with the Archetype or Idea. This means that traditional aesthetics is a 'style of expression', a 'style of life', a 'way of being'. It seeks to make the spirit sensitive to the universal Beauty which is the expression of the principial Artist or Architect.

According to the primordial Tradition, art is a *search*, a vertical leap to gain the True and the Beautiful, and, at the same time, it is a horizontal manifestation to reveal the geometrical proportions of luminous tones.

The artist of the philosophy of becoming arouses sensory pleasure; the artist of the Philosophy of Being awakens Harmony with universal life.

From the traditional perspective, every form/body is seen as a structure which releases the Beauty of the Idea. Someone who *contemplates* through the form sees the sublime Beauty of the archetypal geometry of Being. Form supports the contemplation of the Intelligible and hence supports the ascension to the Harmony and Beauty which are within us. Art conceived in this way is a pathway of realisation, a 'Way of Beauty' which leads to the supreme Beauty which is supreme Perfection.

Anyone who follows this Way will gradually be able to perceive and contemplate Beauty, Harmony, and Accord, which are revealed through the beauty, harmony, and accord of the forms/volumes. Art must nourish the body and the soul of the contemplator. Plato, Plotinus, and others point to art precisely as a Way of realisation.

The true artist makes visible the Invisible and guides the pulsating heart of the beholder to the attainment of the Invisible; he is the Master, just as the *Kṣatriya* is Master of the military *art*. Hence there is initiation with regard to the order of Trades and Art.

Love, too, is a Way of realisation, and in this sense is an art of *contemplation*.

Q. I have read a few pages of 'The Threefold Pathway of Fire' which strike me as relevant to what we are saying; or rather, I must say that I have a better understanding of their meaning. Are some of the aphorisms trying to give this sort of stimulus?

R. Yes. Some chapters in particular, if read with proper attention, can give the right stimulus.[1] When we speak of Accord, Harmony, Love, and so on, it is always with reference to becoming commensurate with the universal

---

[1] See in particular 'All-pervasive Fire or Realisation through Love of the Beautiful' in *The Threefold Pathway of Fire*, by Raphael. Aurea Vidyā, New York.

Order. The 'chaotic movement' of individuality needs to come into accord and harmonise itself with the universal Order. To love the Principle means to be in accord with universal Life.

Q. (Penultimate questioner) – So if I have understood correctly, the art of the Philosophy of Being is not produced as a function of enjoyment or sensory pleasure?

R. No, not at all. When art loses its cathartic and transforming function, it abandons itself to the exaltation of emotional/sentimental aesthetics as an end in itself. In the same way, when religion loses touch with the transcendent sphere, it contents itself with offering purely emotional comfort. When politics loses sight of universal *Dharma*, it resolves into a self-assertive demagogy in order to enlarge the ego and the instinctive thirst for power of an individual or of several people. When the social Orders lose sight of the Principle from which they have emerged, there can be nothing but class warfare. What is often defined as the 'sensitivity' of the individual is nothing but an animal/instinctive 'reaction'. Plants, and even minerals, have this kind of sensitivity. But art must not aim to arouse *reaction*, but *action* which promotes Accord, Harmony, and Beauty.

+ Harmony/Beauty which is always understood as commensurate with the archetype?

R. Yes, as we have already said. Harmony means vibrating in union with Idea, being commensurate with the Principle, making the Archetype and the prototype an expressive harmonious *unity*. Art is work which conforms to the Order. All this is the fruit of *intuition* and *contemplation*.

Music can also be considered from this viewpoint. Plato says:

'And Harmony, which has a similar motion to that of the soul, which lives within us, must not constitute – for anyone who is availing himself of the Muses by means of the intellect – a source of vain pleasures, because Harmony has been given by the Muses to order and put into agreement with itself the soul's motion, which has become inharmonious; and in the same way rhythm, which in us is devoid of measure and grace, was given by the Muses to the same end.'[1]

Pythagoras based Philosophy on the law of Harmony.

+ This means that the artist has great responsibilities within society?

R. Certainly. In the society of Being it is not only the artist who has clear-cut responsibilities (we have said that the artist who has *realised* this Art is a Master), but all the members of the social body, because, in brief, they express themselves by means of an art.

Social life based on the Philosophy of Being is motivated by *right action*[2], which also corresponds to the inclination inherent in the *guṇas*, while the society of becoming is motivated and driven merely by activism, quantitative production, and ruthlessness in business *affairs*.

The former inclines upwards, only to come down again later and unfold the Idea; this means that *right action* is first and foremost the result of contemplation. The latter,

---

[1] Plato, *Timaeus*, 47d.

[2] To go deeper into this topic see *Bhagavadgītā*, with the Commentary of Raphael. Aurea Vidyā.

being conditioned by the ego and the individualistic urge, tends towards 'doing for the sake of doing', towards action, self-satisfaction, rather then realisation of the Self.

From the view of Being *everything* is to be done with Art. From this come the 'composure', 'dignity', and 'detachment' which are required in the action. An entrepreneur (*Vaiśya*) who is identified with his work and the fruits of his work, such as money, is not in harmony with the Idea, does not accomplish the 'right action', does not live with *art*, with *composure*, and does not live up to the Philosophy of Being.

+ You often use these words, too, in the book 'The Threefold Pathway of Fire'. Are they therefore related to this art?

R. Yes. There is an art even in dying as the ego. The 'Way of Fire' is a *sādhanā*, or way (ὸδός) in Parmenides, which is practised with 'composure', 'boldness' and 'right action'.[1]

Q. We are talking of art, harmony, and beauty, but life nowadays is unfortunately characterised by violence and consumer ruthlessness at all levels. This disturbs the *sādhanā*.

R. I think so, too. Violence is the result of animal reaction. We must find the courage to free ourselves from the projections of the hidden persuaders.

Q. And yet there were violence and even bloody sacrifices in the traditional civilisations. How do you explain this fact?

---

[1] See 'Sulphurous Dignity' in *The Threefold Pathway of Fire*, by Raphael. Aurea Vidyā, New York.

R. We are speaking of the Vision of the Being. We have said that there have always been deteriorations, unfortunately, and not only in the religious sphere. But it is important to distinguish a deterioration of a vision from the Vision itself, which transcends all conflict and egoic imperfection. Let us remind ourselves that the dark age began a long time ago.

Today we live in a chaotic blur of activity because man has gradually lost the Vision as well as contemplation; he has lost the true Art, the only one which can lead him to harmony and to the transcendence of the sensory realm.

Q. (First questioner). So do all the activities in the society of Being tend to stimulate the harmony of the Soul? Do they have an educational validity of spiritual growth?

R. Most of the activities of the society of becoming are promoted by the egoic mind, and so it's a question of activities which are born and die in the realm of the individualised.

A society whose operations are completely taken up within a single aspect of the *totality* of Being cannot but be lame and partial.

Every activity motivated by the ego and accomplished for the ego is characterised by violence, rivalry, profit, pride, utilitarian ethics, and hedonism. Unless man subordinates his actions to the Principle, he will find himself, sooner or later, in mental confusion and social disorder. If action doesn't go towards the Truth, it degenerates into *activism*, with all the consequences that can follow from that. Society nowadays is experiencing the results of this. We said that the entrepreneur (*Vaiśya*), like the employee (*Śūdra*), the politician (*Kṣatriya*), and so on, must think of work as a means of elevation and emancipation. From this perspective, there can be no exploitation or coercion, because everyone is in his right place. In the *Gītā*, Arjuna has to fight (engage in action) for a precise universal *Dharma*, not for himself as 'ego', and not to acquire wealth or kill another out of desire for power.[1]

Q. So action is not rejected by the Philosophy of Being?

R. Action has its function. It is not action in itself which hinders realisation.

The Philosophy of Being has no part in restless activism, the desire to do for the sake of doing, that egoistic and imprisoning movement. Contemplation and action are two activities of the spirit with their own directions. They are not opposed to each other. Whether to follow one or the other depends on personal 'vocation'.

Beyond these two activities, however, there is Being, whose state cannot be described either in terms of contemplation or in terms of action.

Q. Excuse me if I make this observation: even with regard to these two, some people will come to blows in an effort to show the superiority of one over the other, whatever the case may be.

R. Why interpret life, with its varied expressions, in terms of superiority and inferiority?

Contemplation and action represent a polarity. I would dare to add that they are mere verbal concepts.

---

[1] To go deeper into this aspect, see the 'Preface' by Raphael to the *Bhagavadgītā*, particularly the short Chapter '*Kṣatriya* Initiation'. Aurea Vidyā, New York.

In the realm of the manifest, everything is action or movement: it's simply that action accomplished at the non-formal or principial plane is different from action accomplished at the formal plane. We could say that they are two expressions of consciousness which are certainly not equal, though they are not opposed to each other or mutually exclusive.

However, you who are more inclined to Realisation than to defending egoic preferences, try to perceive Harmony everywhere. It is only the mind which interprets things in terms of higher and lower, large and small, major and minor, commander and subaltern. Wars often begin in defence of a principle of superiority.

Q. You spoke about intuition and contemplation. What do you mean by these words?

R. I mean that intuition which ranges freely beyond the sensible and beyond discursive speech, and which puts its roots down into the principial eternal.

Contemplation is something more. It corresponds to *samādhi* in *Vedānta*. To contemplate is to 'see', and it corresponds to Plato's *theoria* (θεορία).

Q. (First questioner). Is the artist a creator or an imitator? I hope my friends will pardon me, but I should like to ask them not to depart from the subject of art.

R. According to the Philosophy of Being, the activity of the artist resolves into perceiving the 'models' of Being and 'manifesting' them by means of a support, a form of expression. This is an act of intuition and creation.

Within Himself God conceived just ideas and created them. The artist does the same: he perceives the Ideas *within himself* and creates the appropriate medium of manifestation. To re-discover the Beautiful, the Soul must not look outside, must not become extrovert, but by abstracting itself from the sensible it must go back within itself and in this way perceive the Accord/Harmony which is consubstantial with its own nature.

The philosophy of becoming, by contrast, thinks of art as imitation or re-creation of the *forms* of nature, according to the individual style of the artist. In other words, the artist looks outside himself rather than within himself, and he fixes his eyes only on the 'copies' of Reality, the lifeless 'shadows'.

With the former vision he is free at the formal creative plane, while with the latter he is always conditioned by nature which is already 'formed' and objectivised.

+ But he is still imitating the world of Ideas.

R. In order not to make use of the world of Ideas, the artist would have to position himself outside the nature of Being, which is clearly impossible.

We insist on saying that he is on a par with the great Architect or divine Artist, but he cannot put himself outside or above Reality.

It must be added that, generally speaking, profane art does not communicate Ideas, but simply arouses mere excitations or emotional stimuli, and some which are often also instinctive. Television, cinema, and literature itself generally represent instruments which provoke instinctive and emotional reactions. Every item is 'created' to arouse pleasure, and hence sensations, rather than Ideas and principles. And by not going beyond the rational human being, art consequently becomes individualist and limited by space and time.

All individual exhibitionism should be excluded from art. The initiated artist, and this includes the *Ṛṣi* and the Realised Man, expresses himself anonymously. By means of art and with right contemplation and action, he reveals the True/Beautiful.

The Beautiful, of course, is not that which pleases the senses, and the Just is not that which the ego can conceive in its personal, contingent, and utilitarian evaluation (one should meditate on this).

So by 'sensitivity' we do not mean emotional/reactive sensitivity, but sensitivity to the Intelligible.

The ego evaluates in terms of pleasure/displeasure, attraction/repulsion, but it is not under such conditions that we can 'create' and hence give proper stimulation.

+ Can every disciple be an artist?

R. Certainly. Plotinus states that the one who contemplates 'offers himself, one might say, as material, allowing himself to be fashioned into the form of what is seen; and then alone is he potentially himself.'[1]

The greatest masterpiece of life is represented by this movement of realisation. The Idea is Being; Beauty is the innermost Truth which fashions all things and to which every Soul profoundly aspires. Every human explicative activity represents an arrow aimed at this single target. If the arrow is deflected, the action becomes chaotic, unproductive, and vain.

---

[1] Plotinus, *Enneads*, IV, IV, 2.

Truly 'original' action draws its inspiration from the Origin, the Norm, the Principle, the supreme Knowledge (*Cit*).

+ Should art express Knowledge? I don't understand this final concept.

R. If art is inherent in man, it must reveal Knowledge, which represents an aspect of Being, rather than feeling and pleasure, which are characteristic of the sensory functions.

If feeling is involved, this is just an accident.

+ From what we are saying, may it be inferred that in art the content has a principal, essential function?

R. Man is *Noûs* (intellect, not to be confused with *manas* or *diánoia*). It is therefore his task to reveal noetic contents clothed in appropriate forms.

The proportion or Harmony which he must realise between Idea and expression is the work of art. From this it also follows that art must express the True, which is, in fact, relevant to the *noésis* of man.

+ From this point of view, must the artist be realised? Should he also be spiritually prepared?

R. Art is not cut off from realisation; rather it is a means to it. Every action must tend to the realisation of the individual (τέλος).

It is therefore necessary to distinguish between technical or skilful ability pure and simple and the effective realisation of contemplating and then fashioning. It is not enough to be good with words to be a poet of the temper, say, of Dante.

\+ I think that with this kind of art one can lose what is called artistic spontaneity.

R. Not really. Creation always remains an act which is free, spontaneous, and innocent. Bear in mind that it is always the artist who contemplates and who fashions the forms.

\+ Can we define this kind of art as metaphysical?

R. We would say that we find ourselves facing an art whose contents are of a universal and principial order, not profane and not an imitation of something 'natured' or *objectified*.
  Every work of art develops around a 'seed' (music has its theme around which the musical structure is created), which should be of a transcendental order but it is brought into our three-dimensional world by the artist and hence is clothed with a suitable form or body. In our world we can perceive and comprehend only by means of concepts and forms. If the seed comes from the eternal, then the painting, the sculpture, and so on, are immortal.

\+ But isn't this how things normally work?

R. The intuition of the artist, of which we are speaking in general terms, is a subconscious intuition. His inspiration is of a sensory order, brought to maturity in the environment of 'emotional feeling'.
  In traditional portraiture, on the other hand, the aim is to catch the expressive *quality* of the subject, the *function* determined by the *guṇas*, the dynamic aspect of the soul

which is seeking to manifest itself. The icon of Christ frequently represents, not a faithful portrayal of his features, but what Christ can demonstrate in his living, dynamic, and vital condition. The *Śakti*, or nature, is caught in its 'creative' aspect, in its 'naturing' state, while profane art catches nature in its 'natured'[1], objective, static, and dead state.

+ So in this way do we have a portrait of the soul rather than of the body?

R. In a certain sense, yes, because the body is nothing but a mere instrument by means of which the true, real man is seeking to express himself.

So if one wishes to paint or sculpt a person's face, for example, there are two possible approaches. The first consists principally in catching the *daímon* (δαίμων) which is behind the mask/face. This means catching the true, real, and essential man in his creative dimension. The other approach consists in catching only the mask/face, the static likeness, devoid of life and devoid of divine Eros. Sometimes in the mask, or photograph, one may detect the psychological frame of mind, but it always remains within the individual.

If by 'real' we mean that which underlies forms, we shall have to deduce that the art of the Philosophy of Being is 'realist'. A temple, as traditionally conceived, although it is located in time and space, can transport the 'contemplator' beyond time and space. At most, and from this perspective, we can say that art is a raft which

---

[1] See note on page 33.

takes the individual into the world of Meanings, Causes, Principles, Ideas, and supra-individual Reality.

As we can observe, art in the individualised world has an essential function and a stimulating power which can bring about *samādhi*, ecstasy.

+ Must I deduce, therefore, that art, as we normally think of it, reproduces or re-creates illusions, illusory forms, items which are *māyā*? In short, is the artist merely taking *photographs* of *māyā*?

R. We can only say that art, as it is normally thought of, draws the attention to 'husks' devoid of soul (consider 'still life' works), and is used to give a realistic picture but not to create. The art of the Philosophy of Being, on the other hand, focuses on the life which animates these husks. This means, as we have already noted, that a vase, a piece of music, a portrait, or a temple constructed according to the canons of Art put the viewer/listener in touch with universal reality and transmit energies, influences capable of producing specific effects in the heart of the contemplator. Such a 'creation' is an instrument which resonates with universal cosmic life.

+ I should like to put a final question. I see that some friends are growing impatient; I suppose they wish to speak. However, I must say that this question is not mine, but was put to me a little while ago.

The question is this: is the artist a privileged person, a being with greater endowments than others?

R. There are no individuals who are higher or lower than others. There are people who are qualified to undertake specific tasks. Even to be an agricultural labourer requires particular qualifications and aptitudes which are always inherent in the *guṇas*.

A true farmworker must have a strong sensitivity to the energy rhythms of the planet earth, the vital rhythms of other planets and those of the soil. He must know how to arrange the plants themselves in a harmonious way. He must have an adequate knowledge of astrology and a love which must be *perceived* by the plants and the environment. He must also know the psychology of animals; he must know how to intuit the 'correct completion' of the work, because he has to be in the 'right relationship' with the surrounding nature. The technological agricultural worker of the society of hyper-exploitation uses only violence on the clod of earth, on the plants, and even on the animals; he is therefore not an Artist. In what sense may an artist of agriculture be inferior to others? What matters is that each should properly fulfil his own *dharma*, his own duty.

Q. So are there no masters and servants, no exploiters and exploited, no racist swine and slaves, no corrupt people and none that are oppressed?

R. I see that you are always preoccupied with this problem.

+ I have good reasons, believe me; but it's not a question of going into details. I am neither a reactionary nor an emotional fanatic. I tell you that I have had my experiences, apart from the fact that history can teach us a great deal.

R. My brother, what can I say to you? It seems to me that something has come out of our conversations which may help you to understand the problem. To you, then, I have already given some specific answers.

Master and slave[1] are concepts created by the domineering, exclusivist individuality which thirsts for compensations. In undivided Being there are no dualities, there are no distinctions, there are no masters and servants. Do you understand? If, in the course of time and in every field of human experience, there have been solipsistic exploiters and dictators, this does not mean that such distortions cannot be corrected.

+ In short, the *pariah*, the exploited, the disinherited, who have been made like this by the Prince: are they, or are they not, within Being like everyone else?

R. If the *pariah* were outside Being, he would be another Being, and two Absolutes cannot co-exist. To attribute such worth to him, then, would mean endowing him with a greatness which not even the *Brāhmaṇa* or the realised philosopher possesses.

Q. Allow me to say, however, that in the world of becoming there are ignorant people who walk under the guidance of their feet rather than their heads, and we cannot leave them out of account.

R. Ignorance and knowledge originate from the same matrix. All dreaming souls are a combination of the two.

---

[1] See 'Freedom and slavery' in *At the Source of Life*, by Raphael. Aurea Vidyā, New York.

We have said that every being is the product of the inter-relationship of the *guṇas*, an inter-relationship which the being itself has determined, which simply means that the inter-relationship is not absolute.

There is nothing higher or lower, large or small – from certain standpoints there is not even the sacred and the profane, because these are always related to points of view – but there are *qualities* which are expressed through an instrument or a body of manifestation. In other words, *nature* is revealed through unnumbered modalities of existence, all of which go back into the organisation and harmony of life.

SECOND PART

SHADOWS CAST ON GURUS
AND ON TRADITIONAL CULTURALISTS

Q. I acknowledge the validity of certain theses and a great many statements, but it is difficult to harmonise one's own life with that of someone who, unfortunately, states different things and starts off from opposite points of view. In fact, philosophy nowadays is of another order that is mechanistic, phenomenalistic, and historicist. The philosophical reality of today becomes and flows; it's continually moving and changing; and this has been stated by other friends. There is no dialogue with my fellowman: for him, reality is objective, external, and perpetually changing; for me, things are different.

It is sad that we don't understand each other, and it is tiring to fight a majority which chooses to put limits on itself.

Life is made even more difficult by the conduct of some *gurus* (instructors) who offer knowledge and celestial happiness as if they were giving away peanuts. Some of them even become rich by cashing in on many people's innocence, and this creates further chaos and mistrust. Moreover, one can observe that Western spirituality is exploited for political ends.

Most of our national esoteric and spiritual periodicals, and others of this kind, do not depart from a custom, which has become a system: arguing and disputing, in addition to living on memories, on the past, on things which are no longer, on a mere *history* of the tradition. What can you say to me about this state of affairs?

R. I appreciate your confusion and your concern. From certain points of view, I cannot fail to recognise what you are saying. To answer your questions would require an entire book. You are saying things that are specific, serious and delicate, but unfortunately, within certain limits, I have to say that you are right. I say 'unfortunately' because I would prefer not to know about certain facts. You are expecting a reply, and I don't know where to begin.

+ Please say something to me, because I need to re-discover a balance and a proper relationship with my spiritual life. I don't believe I'm the only one who needs this. I think others have the same problem. I personally know some who have been deeply disconcerted by certain attitudes.

R. As far as concerns the philosophical conception of today, according to which 'everything flows and becomes', there is nothing to worry about. It is a philosophical view like so many others, and we accept it as such. Of course, it isn't new, because Heraclitus, back in 520 B.C., was, in fact, saying that 'everything is in flux', and that we cannot step into the same water twice.

On the other hand, this conception is not completely wrong. Phenomenal truth is accepted, for example, even by *Vedānta*, which calls it *śakti, prakṛti, māyā*, and so on; it's just that *Vedānta* has gone beyond phenomenal 'truth' to reveal an intelligible reality of an unconditioned and permanent order within which every phenomenal 'truth' is reintegrated.[1]

It is not a question of clashing or for us to expect acknowledgements and agreements. What we can do is not to accept the imposition of certain philosophies by force and violence. As long as we are in a philosophical and dialectical context, we are happy to share spontaneous urges of inquiry, even if they lead to different positions. What matters is that every serious search should be undertaken with complete freedom of expression and dignified emulation. Plato would say, 'Sameness in diversity'.

A philosophical vision must not proclaim exclusivism and unilateralism. It must only enunciate, explain, and engage in dialogue. For us seekers, therefore, as for all true seekers of every order and degree, it is appropriate to face one another in freedom and with mutual respect. A philosophy which tries to impose itself by force is no longer a philosophy (a friend of Knowledge), but a demagogy, the egoic tyranny of a person, a group, or an entire social class.

We must uphold the right to be free to declare a philosophy of life based on certain postulates and specific experiences of consciousness, a right which we must also allow to those who may disagree with us. The fact that most people have and follow a particular philosophy of life is not important. We are not saying that Truth has to belong to the majority: far from it.

What is important is for each of us to enquire carefully, discriminate peacefully, gather evidence freely in order to

---

[1] To go deeper into the three stages or levels of reality as contemplated by *Vedānta*, see 'Real and unreal' in *The Pathway of Non-Duality*, by Raphael. Aurea Vidyā, New York.

discover the ultimate goal of existence, the very source of life. Let us bear in mind that we are speaking of 'realisative philosophy' and therefore of a philosophy which leads to self-transfiguration. This is the true Philosophy of Being, with a capital 'P'.

We know that those who follow the philosophy of becoming, the philosophy of the ego, live the materialistic philosophical postulates in practical life. We must acknowledge, by way of contrast, that the followers – but certainly not all – of the Philosophy of Being neither live nor live up to their philosophical vision. This also gives many phenomenalists – if we may use such a term – the opportunity to write things that are unedifying, often exaggerated, and deliberately contrived about both the Philosophy of Being and its upholders.[1]

At this point, however, it would be right for us to say some words of disapproval not only with regard to shallow instructors but also with regard to aspirants who are unprepared and uninformed.

If one may speak of a fault, it applies to both sets. The first, being sufficiently cultured, possessing specific 'psychological techniques' but not *effective* Realisation, and being absorbed by the 'system', indulge in thoughts that are particularly of a financial nature. But what can one do if the life of *māyā* offers these opportunities? In good or bad faith, there are speculators in all fields, profane and otherwise, even at the scientific level. The second, being disinclined to think, search, and understand, yield themselves as things to the first bidder who can promise quick results, easy experiences of enlightenment, and transcendence at the drop of a hat.

---

[1] See Plato, *Politéia*, VI, 489d.

Aspirants who are devoid of all qualifications, eager for psychic, rather than spiritual, results or for psychological peace, having minds that are totally inert, and being allergic to reading and self-knowledge, cannot help meeting that guru who is suited to them.

When there are novices who are ready to sell themselves in order to acquire a modest psychic power offered by some master, even at exorbitant prices, it means that they have understood very little, and ignorance is costly.

It would be good practice to try to understand whether a seeker is motivated by mere psychological problems, by philosophical urges, or by a mystical calling. The direction changes according to his problem, as do those who should help him. But many *gurus*, wishing to 'save the world', make indiscriminate offers of easy initiation, by organising mass *festivals* so as to create emotional conditionings and subconscious exchange of devotional fanaticism which will then have a negative impact on the self-awareness of the individuals.

If there are speculators in every field of human activity, it is because there are people ready to support them and even idolise them.

There have always been domineering people and dictators, because there have always been people who have unconsciously looked for dictators and exploiters.

There are aspirants who go searching, not for Knowledge, *which is within them*, but for wonder-workers, prophets, people who can transport them bodily to paradise, instructors who guarantee success and a solution to their everyday worries.

There are false *gurus* because there are false disciples. The most difficult thing which I have personally encountered in relation to many aspirants is getting them to reflect, to discriminate, to think rightly and even independently.

Most want freedom for *the ego*, not freedom *from the ego*. They want an easy technique for reaching *nirvāṇa* quickly. It also happens that some are looking in some teaching for an excuse to perpetuate their incompleteness and their escapes.

It is not easy to propose seeking the Truth, because, in general, most people are thirsting for mere mystery, gratification of the ego and not for the death of the ego.[1]

Q. But hasn't it been often said that one needs to realise oneself rather than read? What use can mere reading be?

R. Precisely. Superficial reading and merely memorising the teaching are of no use. We are speaking of enquiry, study, meditation, intellectual and intuitive penetration of the Texts and the Teachings; of evaluation and subsequent experience.

To read Plotinus just to learn some doctrines, to become learned and make a show of being cultured is one story; to meditate, comprehend, exert oneself to penetrate the truth which the words conceal, and live the truths that have been garnered is another story. This is how it still is with the Christian scriptures, the Buddhist scriptures, and others.

I would ask you to consider that the mind is one of the instruments of being, and is neither better nor worse than the others. It is a vehicle, an instrument, and no more, and every instrument can be used properly or improperly. It

---

[1] See 'Realization and Psychological Comfort' in Essence and Purpose of Yoga, by Raphael. Elements Books. ...

is not by ignoring a vehicle, even the physical one, that we put ourselves in the right position to approach the *sādhanā*. Our instruments of expression are valid and of great assistance if we know how to use them appropriately.

We start off from an intra-individual condition, and thought is a valid support; to reject it completely can mean falling into apathy and psychical quietism, or into slavery to a self-assertive 'master'.

The mind, suitably stimulated, catches its higher octave, which is the intellect, pure reason, super-conscious intuition. Being, in fact, an instrument, the mind serves a purpose and hence is not an end in itself. Just as we don't live merely to nourish the physical body, but we nourish ourselves in order to realise the end of living, in the same way we mustn't make use of the mental body merely to amass ideas upon ideas to the point of satiety. Let us bear in mind that we are dealing with self-realisation, which means that it is the individual himself who must find, within himself, what he really is. All the sacred Texts aim precisely at re-awakening to this Reality, which is one throughout all that exists. Knowledge does not create truth/reality, but dispels error.

A mind that is greedy for ideas, representations, accumulated learning is the equivalent of that guzzling physical body which gobbles food out of greed for gobbling it.

Eating, at the physical or mental level, serves no purpose unless the food is chewed, swallowed, assimilated, and transformed into the blood of life and the consciousness of Being.

An idea which does not transform itself into the reality of life is only an obstruction. Individuals who have great erudition measured by quantity and who have refined their mental, psychical power believe that they are superior to others and that they have realised something, and yet they have realised very little; they have filled the belly of their mind with food without any assimilation, synthesis, or transfiguration.

Wisdom and erudition are different things, and anyone who approaches the Philosophy of Being must remember this. A true Philosopher is a friend and seeker of eternal, universal Wisdom. Traditional Knowledge aims at Wisdom, not at erudition or the quantisation of cognitions about the world of names and forms.

Although the mind is relative, it is a vehicle which, if rightly used, leads to the achievement of certain steps but which, if wrongly used, can be an obstacle for oneself and cause harm to others.

Q. Then what can I do to understand myself and grow in this chaos of techniques, *mantras*, *sādhanās*, and *gurus*, in this society of mystical preachers and politicians, in this world in which 'materialistic' *gurus* and supporters of *carpe diem* deceive you with paradise on earth, and spiritual *gurus* with paradise in heaven?

Nowadays we have to be on our guard against three types of *guru*: the political, who wants to subjugate you with the mirage of social justice; the missionary mystic, who wants to deceive you with the mirage of heavenly justice; and finally the culturalist, who sells you, at very high prices, mere words and chatter which take you away from the essence and simplicity of the Truth.

Many young people, including me, feeling frustrated and taken for a ride, are knocked from pillar to post by these *gurus*. How can we free ourselves from political, religious, hot-air, consumeristic fanaticism?

R. I appreciate your urge to wake up and your thirst for a solution to the fundamental problems of life.

If you wish to *aim* at *being*, if you wish to aim at discovering the world of principles, you have to begin by reading, meditating on, and reflecting on some of the Teachings from East and West, because the Truth, with a capital 'T', is everywhere and stands outside space and individuality. Thus you can study the philosophy of Parmenides, Plato, and Plotinus; you can meditate on *Qabbālāh*; or on *Vedānta*, *Sāṁkhya*, the Christian Gospels, and other works. But you must make a deep study of these philosophies, ponder, take notes, copy out intuitions; you must commit yourself fully and give yourself up to the search, but with great humility and without preconceptions.

Pure enquiry stands outside *a priori* considerations. Go to the direct source and don't yield to intermediaries. But pursue this work with active consciousness, as an intelligent seeker and investigator.

+ This research work will occupy me for several years, and how can I get there by myself? Although I myself am the true *guru*, I need a guide to begin with.[1]

R. You must make the effort. You must develop intuition. If your enquiry is serious, if your offering to Knowledge is devoid of false superimpositions, you are not alone. A true seeker of truth, although alone, is never alone. You will forgive me this apparent contradiction.

---

[1] See particularly the beginning of 'Name, form and *vāsanā*' in *Beyond Doubt*, by Raphael. Aurea Vidyā, New York.

Of course, time is needed, especially at the beginning, in order to find and assimilate particular things, but do we wish to fall into one of those errors that we spoke about just now?

Do you want an easy Teaching? Realisation within easy reach? Do you believe, perhaps, that Liberation is obtained by going to an *āśram* in your spare time or reading a book at bedtime when you are already tired? Do you believe that this kind of enquiry can be carried out merely in work breaks or by leafing through a text in the car while waiting at a red traffic-light?

Porphyry tells us that Plotinus listened tirelessly to his *guru* Ammonius Saccas for eleven years; and Porphyry himself was a disciple of Plotinus for many a year. Many *gurus* in India – and there are true *gurus*, believe me – have lived for ten, fifteen, thirty years in retirement, in meditation, engaging in sacrifices of every kind.

+ You see, our work and life in the West don't let us have much time at our disposal. Unfortunately, this is a great obstacle.

R. Then, like good Westerners who are efficient at the teaching level, we could invent push-button realisation. Doesn't it already happen with horoscopes? Joking apart, I appreciate this difficulty. However, I think that an individual who is thirsty for Liberation will manage to find enough time and space. I repeat: help cannot fail to be present for anyone who is seeking the Truth and not mystery or psychic phenomena.

SCOURGERS AND EXECUTIONERS

Q. One day one of my brothers on the path was insulted by a group of fanatical spiritualists with specious and even false arguments. Faced with this attack, I am extremely perplexed.

Recently I was also involved in a great controversy with a vicious culturalist. Without going any further into it, I should like to understand two things. Why does a critical and reactive dialectic arise? What is the proper standpoint of consciousness to adopt with regard to an insult?

R. The world of the ego is the world of opposition, reaction, criticism, polemics, and dogmatic and demagogic exclusivism.[1] Some write about spirituality and even metaphysics with a consciousness that is almost counter-traditional.

Although they claim to abhor sentiments, they are on the plane of disorderly reaction, which is precisely 'feeling' or sentiment.

Q. From past experience, I too am convinced that some are restless and they fight others because they haven't yet

---

[1] See 'Points of view and erudition' in *Beyond Doubt*, by Raphael. Aurea Vidyā, New York.

found peace within themselves. It is a retaliation of the ego; or rather, I'd say, of a mind that is not wisely directed.

Would you agree if I said in these examples the mind plays a determining role?

R. A soul at peace has comprehended Truth in its entirety; and someone who has *comprehended* has transcended every possible duality and phenomenal polarity.

The mental faculty, or the objectivising empirical mind, if properly exercised, becomes a *psychical power*[1] which some use both rightly and wrongly. Although they seem to loathe psychical powers, they fail to realise that it is precisely through them that they are nourishing and expressing themselves. We know that at the level of the empirical mind white can become black and black, white. With the mind we can *demonstrate* whatever we choose, but Truth is that which is. Let us repeat: some 'direct' the mind towards goals of 'attack', reaction, and vindictive acrimony. They make use of dialectic, and proof at any cost, of the authoritative 'I distinguish', of the effective quip, of essays that can even be offensive, and so on; and dragged along by the 'power' itself, they give themselves up to world of mere reaction, forgetting not only the 'initiatory Dignity of the *Kṣatriya*' – which requires measured action, fair fighting, and calm discussion – but even good manners and proper conduct.

There is no doubt that if all the energy were employed in attempting *to be* rather than in creating mental reactions, the individual would benefit. If he were to fight his own

---

[1] For 'psychical powers', see 'The *siddhis*' in *The Pathway of Non-Duality*, by Raphael. Aurea Vidyā, New York.

imperfection instead of fighting other people, we would have more Saints and fewer executioners.

The feeling of separatism and self-assertion, which are camouflaged by a thousand sophistries, and emotional fanaticism which is masked by verbose rationalism have never performed any useful services - quite the reverse.

Humanity has greater need of Realised Men than of sophists, wranglers, and dogmatic, authoritarian theologians, especially nowadays. Words of sophistry do nothing but feed ignorance. Unfortunately, at the level of mind the winner is the one who has the greater 'vocabulary' and more arguments, knows how to play with words and sophistries and how to hatch concepts (from which comes 'power'). We mustn't forget that, according to the *truth*, 'conceptual proof' that others *are not* doesn't count; what counts is 'proof through living' – and first of all for oneself – what one *is*. And when one is, the mind falls silent and thought comes to an end, but there is also an end to the purpose for which so many *individualities* live and continue to live on the borders of a useless and vain spiritual culturalism.

Anyone who views metaphysics not as a verbal concept but as an expression of living reality, in what sense and from what perspective could he have a 'feeling' of opposition, reaction, recrimination, rancour, or resentment?

In the One-without-a-second the objectivising and egoistic mind no longer exists; nor is there another person who can be blamed.

You see, there are principally two ways to maintain that one *is the only person* to possess the Truth and the instruments fit to make it germinate in others. The first is by 'affirming', the second is by 'negating'. One can *affirm* one's own exclusivist authority, directly and peremptorily, by focusing only on oneself. Alternatively, one can try to annihilate and negate all possible rivals. In other words, by demolishing and negating all the others one ends up by being the *only one left* on the battlefield; that is, one applies *neti neti*, at the level of the ego, unfortunately: a paradox of egoic intelligence.

Through the method of *neti neti*, *Vedānta* excludes all that *is not* (*māyā*) in order to actually reach what *is* (*ātman*).

Well now, some people, consciously or unconsciously – it comes to the same thing – negate and exclude the various rivals (the mind thinks, 'In truth he is not, he is not') so fully that they are the only ones left. And this is what the ego wants: to be the only, absolute, and undisputed arbiter; to be the only actor and recite monologues on the great stage of the world. This can also be extended to some spiritual and absolutist political religions.

With the first way of working we have self-assertion through isolation (no account is taken of others); with the second we have self-assertion by means of an eristic process, exclusive and humiliating sophistry, and annihilation of others. This second way is worse than the first.

At certain levels the second is killed physically and with crude methods (we are already acquainted with this brutal way of doing things). At other levels people are killed through a scathing mind. But it's the same thing; or rather, death by the axe of *manas* (the mind) is more sadistic, even though it appears less brutal.

The 'will to kill' is objectified, expressed, revealed, and the *ego-child* is sadistically gratified, lives on, and grows.

An animal attacks out of hunger, but man/the individual, putting on the face of an angel, attacks for the pleasure of attacking. Physical or mental attack is always the result of some incompleteness, a physical lacuna, some frustration, something unresolved in the subconscious, some fanaticism. There is nothing worse than setting oneself up as a judge, an arbiter, a defender, an executioner. There is nothing worse than wielding the man-slaying axe in the name of an 'explanatory contribution', in the name of the '*dharma* to defend at all costs', the need to 'prove', the 'mission' to whip.

Truth has no need of proofs or preachers. It reveals itself and proves itself by itself to anyone who is ready to receive it.

Someone who *is* simply reveals the Truth, and that is sufficient. Someone who *is* does not even ask himself whether to act or not act, to 'save' or 'prove', defend or attack, be this or that.

Someone who *is* lives only in perfection and fullness, and is above insult and praise, even above good and evil, beyond all the *gurus* (these are only instruments, and some people, by identifying with them, are engaged in defending the instrument rather than the Teaching). Someone who *is* has stopped opposing because he lives or, better, is in that Unity without a second in which, in fact, there is no shadow of duality or fanaticism.

Well, my dear friends, you are venturing to go by the straight road of realisation of Being and you are not loitering in egoic or psychical realms of the mind which conjure up illusions. Let the wheel of becoming turn round for others, because it is the right *dharma* for them, but you are stopping this wheel and holding fast to the timeless.

+ And what should we do, then, when others act improperly, if they even go so far as a personal attack?

Reaction often attracts reaction, especially when some things occur in an environment where they ought to be considered ridiculous. What could the right level of consciousness be?

R. Isn't it clear from what we have said?

I am not saying 'Turn the other cheek', because such a state of consciousness is very advanced, and misunderstood, but to intervene with composure, dignity, and calmness, and, where possible, to rise above the situation, because on most occasions critical reactions do not even merit a reply. There are certain mental attitudes which are questionable, fanatical, and cynical, and which condemn themselves for what they are, without any specific action in response, without moving, without 'going down' to their level.

René Guénon writes:

> 'Someone who is qualified to speak in the name of a traditional teaching must not debate with the "profane" or indulge in any kind of "polemic". He must simply expound the teaching as it is to those who can comprehend it, at the same time denouncing error wherever it is found and showing it to be such by shining the light of true knowledge upon it. His function is not to start a fight and thus compromise the teaching, but to formulate that concept which he has mastered if indeed he has those principles which must unerringly inspire him. The rule of fighting is the rule of action, and therefore a rule which is individual and transient.

The "unmoving mover" is awake and directs movement without being carried away by it.[1]

+ I remember an aphorism from 'The Way of Fire' which could suit our situation: 'If you are truly on the way of *Vidyā*, you should write on your bedroom wall, "Here one is intent on dying, not on attacking" '.[2]

Q. If you will allow me, I'll take my cue from your sentence: The egoic mind is a psychical power. So, since I have some slight potential for telepathic reception, I am confused when I read, or when people tell me, that telepathic power is an impediment to Realisation. Is that true?

R. Let us not exaggerate. All psychical powers can be obstacles if the *motive* is not in harmony with the discipline that one is undertaking. We would say that it is not the power in itself which imprisons, but the use that is made of it. Mental power, likewise, is not an obstacle, of course, if it is rightly used.

So if you believe it is appropriate, propose this philosophical Ascent with Dignity and innocence, but without expectations. Do not get mixed up in sterile diatribes which only waste energy. Allow each to choose his own path according to his own inclinations and qualifications. A metaphysical way cannot be imposed or be used to proselytise, but is expressed through the Silence which vibrates and awakens.

---

[1] R. Guénon, *La crise du monde moderne*.

[2] See 'The Way of Fire', aphorism 15, in *At the Source of Life*, by Raphael. Aurea Vidyā, New York.

INITIATION AND RITE

Q. For years I have gone around in many different countries looking for someone to give me initiation. I have attended esoteric groups, occult groups, and others, but without success. Finally I met an Indian *Swāmi* who gave me initiation through a specific rite, although I learn from a friend of mine that there is no one today who can give initiation to a Westerner.
 Could you give me some clarification about this? Is it true?

R. Were you more interested in the preparation or in the initiation properly so called?

+ You see, my problem is both complicated and simple at the same time. But I would not like to speak too much about some of my mishaps because they might not be of interest. If you could give me some indications, you would free me from a number of perplexities.

R. I don't see why your initiation should not be valid. Excuse me for asking, but was the *Swāmi* truly a *Swāmi*?

+ Yes. I have also been to his *āśram* in India.

R. And so what are you afraid of? Try to progress with your spiritual discipline and follow the counsels of your Instructor.

+ You see, the friend I was speaking about before tells me that initiation is impossible for a Westerner.

To receive initiation from an Indian *Swāmi* or *Guru* or from a Tibetan *Lama*, he says that one has to be Indian or Tibetan. Since there are no initiatory organisations in the West, every road is obviously blocked to the Western disciple.

R. If I am not mistaken, are you saying that there are national and even regional initiations? That there is Indian initiation, Tibetan initiation, Arabic/Palestinian initiation, African initiation, Italian initiation, and so on? In brief, that the universal becomes racial?

Do you think that initiation is a matter of territory, skin colour, membership of a political or trade-union organisation? Do you think that the true *dīkṣā* is with reference to the social orders considered from the viewpoint of family heredity?

I should not wish you to confuse what is a simple *ceremony* for the admission of an individual to a social organisation, which is, after all, of an order that is external, exoteric, horizontal and specific, with true initiation, which is of a vertical order and has nothing to do with any trades-union or corporate organisations. There are ceremonies of investiture, and there is spiritual Initiation. We should bear in mind, then, that the qualifications of the people belonging to the different social orders are the result of the combinations of the three *guṇas*. In other words, a 'twice-born' is not so because he has received the certificate or testimonial of his order, or because he has been born from a particular parent, but because he possesses those qualifications which correspond to the *guṇas* that make him *truly* what he is. There are 'twice-born' people in the West, even if they don't have the Indian or Tibetan trade-union investiture.

A genius is not so because he has been invested with the title of professor by some university; the investiture may be useful to him simply because it enables him to *practise* his activities within a specific social context, or because it is expressly required of him, but as far as he himself is concerned, he doesn't need bureaucratic certificates.

The Buddha was able to (and actually did) pay no heed to the various social orders because no one could prevent him from being what he truly was. Note that in saying this we have no wish to disregard the functions of the social orders; rather, in this respect, we may say that, although they have been abolished in modern India, no one can annul an individual's *level* of consciousness. We insist, therefore, on the *qualifications*, which are of an order which is inner, vertical, and pertaining to consciousness, rather than on aspects that are outer, horizontal, family-based, and ritualistic.

Let us remember that the spiritual influence is universal, and what matters for its 'descent' is a *prepared consciousness*; the qualifications are therefore those which are required for true Initiation. We should just remember that the Self has no need of initiations or of anything received from *outside*. The energies of *kāma/manas* are the ones to be purified and re-orientated in such a way that the supra-individual influence may touch the embodied reflection of consciousness and re-awaken it. And there are many ways to stimulate the individuality to certain possibilities, and they may not follow common practice. For example, there is a passage in the *Gospels* which has a deeply esoteric connotation: 'Where two or three are gathered together in my name, there am I in the midst.'

A group of qualified people, under certain conditions, can cause the spiritual influence to 'descend' in such a way as to produce specific effects in the consciousness of its members. And this can occur in every geographical region of the planet.

Q. I think many people are entrenched in a theological dogmatism so that they have an excuse for the inability to understand the spirit of certain things. On the other hand, did not Buddha, Jesus, and Śaṅkara himself come to break the dogmas of the Pharisees, the traditionalists, and those with bees in their bonnets about rituals and formality? Moreover, I have known some Western *Swāmis* who have been properly introduced into Indian, and even Tibetan, monastic Orders.

R. At times certain forces in opposition to Initiation indeed try to lead the disciple into a blind alley. With the excuse that one isn't Indian, Arab, or Jewish, these groups, by merely using their mental powers, pin down the disciple who is well-intentioned and sometimes even qualified and make him abandon spirituality. They induce in him a state of distress or a 'complex' about initiation.

+ Are there traditionalists who maintain these things?

R. Not all. In any case the anti-traditional forces are not outside the Tradition, but within it. They are actually the ones that distract and create confusion, especially if they are well taught, if they appeal to the developed *manas* (mind), if they have a rich vocabulary that can make an impression on novices who are still weak, and if they are stubbornly trying to set particular things within fixed, rigid, and formal frameworks.

Q. I have a different problem. I haven't got into the position of being initiated by Eastern Orders, because it strikes me that that would be a betrayal of my spiritual condition as a Westerner.

Is that a mistaken attitude?

R. We need to remember that there is a single Philosophy of being, with different types of adaptation.

Beginning from this principle, there is no reason to exaggerate by making statements of an emotional nature. There may be branches of this Philosophy which conform more or less to our spiritual constitution. If we then note that in the current era some traditional branches, in certain areas of the world, have, for various reasons, lost their effectiveness, it is reasonable to suppose that those who are seeking will have to turn elsewhere. So it's not a question of *abandoning* one's 'faith' but of coming into harmony with that Teaching which is closest to one's own aspirations. It is not necessary to emphasise that we have expressed ourselves in terms of harmonising our consciousness with one traditional branch, and not in terms of mere adherence arising from emotional or intellectual curiosity.

If the principle of the unity of the Teaching[1] were always held in mind, there could be greater spiritual osmosis among the various branches, but unfortunately the fanatics who are attached to the 'letter', the 'form', and the 'region' are always at work defending exclusivity and maintaining that 'mine' is better than 'yours'. To talk of *parochialism* in the context of the Tradition is absurd.

+ Then are initiation and *sādhanā* unnecessary?

R. Let's not go now to the other side of the balance. Extremes don't represent wisdom. Initiation is a reality and has its own specific *raison d'être*. Besides, we are not in the *satya-yuga*, or golden age.

We say, however, 'You are *Brahman*', and the possibilities of the *Brahman* are innumerable. Almost all the initiatory Orders of India and the East in general acknowledge, for example, the *śāmbhavī-dīkṣā*, the initiation given directly by Śiva or Viṣṇu. It is a rare occurrence, but it is possible; it depends on the neophyte's *level* of consciousness. Not all are at the same level of 'wakefulness'. There are some people who 'enter' the human realm with a state of consciousness such that a mere glance from the spiritual Teacher or Master, or an impulse from the environment itself, is sufficient to release within them the supra-individual Influence or spiritual Presence.

It would be useful, however, to give some clarification. In general terms, Initiation in the East happens *directly*, that is, from Master to disciple. A *guru* who has realised universal consciousness (and he must be held to be the

---

[1] To go deeper into this subject, see 'Unity of Tradition' in *Tat Tvam Asi*, by Raphael. Aurea Vidyā, New York.

true *guru*) transmits the influence *directly* to the disciple. But two indispensable pre-requisites are necessary for this to happen: the qualifications of the disciple and the *guru's* state of effective realisation.

'Transmission' can also be effected in time (hence the 'proximity of the Sages' as a factor of realisative *stimulus* that is spoken of in the texts): the qualified disciple gradually attunes himself to the *note* of his *guru*, thereby establishing a kind of umbilical cord through which the Influence circulates and operates.

We are obliged to give just a summary of an entire initiatory process which is very complex, interesting, and beautiful.

Generally speaking, Initiation in the West happens *indirectly*, in the sense that it is an initiatory Institution, functioning normally in its entirety, which gives the Initiation. The Institution is represented by an association of people who, through a particular rite, release certain potentials. We may say that Initiation in the West occurs through a magic-ritualistic act, whereas in the East it is determined by the meeting of 'two qualified hearts', even if the *guru* is always linked to the chain of his predecessors.

As far as the practice and the rite are concerned, they may differ from one organisation to another. Indian, Tibetan, and Western rites may be dissimilar, and it is from this perspective that we may say they differ from one region to another; but the spiritual influence is equal everywhere, and the qualifications which the disciple must have – independently of the form of initiation which he receives – are always the same.

A Masonic rite of initiation is different from one that is Islamic or Jewish or *Vedāntic* or Tibetan or any other, but they all belong to the same Influence, that same *Cit/*

knowledge/consciousness. Being can reveal itself beyond rite, although rite may be appropriate at certain levels and is indispensable at other levels. But what we would like to say above all is this: *prepare yourselves* for the event, acquire the necessary qualifications without beating about the bush, without delay, without being troubled by dogmatists. Prepare the *aura* properly, so that the spiritual Influence may be attracted. Purity of motive, aspiration to transcendence, rising above psychism, and *composure* of consciousness are some of the factors necessary for approaching initiation. This determines the *sympathéia* with the Universal.

Q. In a series of discussions like these, a Tibetan *Lama* said that initiation is the meeting of two minds (Master and disciple). Are you of the same view?

R. Yes. When a certain *tuning* occurs, specific effects are determined in accordance with precise laws.

Q. Forgive me for prolonging the discussion, but there is one thing I would like to say. In what sense can rite be spoken of in the metaphysical realisation of the type known as *Advaita, Asparśa, Zen, Taoist, Platonic*, and so on?

R. Yes, I understand. Let us say in conclusion that the possibilities and ways of realisation are countless, but it is also good to emphasise that a person may be deceived if he believes simplistically that one fine morning he will leap out of bed with his consciousness awakened, just as a person is deceived if he rejects out of hand every form of rite, especially in these dark times.

+ If nothing is ever born and therefore no being exists, and there can be no action, how can we speak of action and rite, initiation and freedom, caste and affiliation?

R. Let us repeat that there are some people who come into the human 'realm' with a special *level* of consciousness.

A re-integrated consciousness has certainly *comprehended*, and someone who has comprehended has come to stillness; for someone who has comprehended, movement has disappeared and motion has ceased. The Self transcends rite, initiations, the social orders, and even liberation.

Q. Please allow me one question; why is the Philosophy of Being eternal and non-human? I don't understand the spirit behind this statement. I hope the friends will forgive my ignorance.

R. If I tell you that before man was born, hydrogen in the sun was already being transformed into helium, do you understand me?

If we say that Being was before empirical man, before all manifestation, this should now be clear for you. Reality, and therefore Truth, is Being itself and thus it is not produced by man, but man can receive it, reveal it, and embody it. This is why we speak of principial, metaphysical Knowledge and *Philosophia perennis*.

You see, all the scientific truths discovered by man already existed. The universal law of gravitation was not invented by Newton: he merely discovered it and revealed it. That law existed even before man was born on this earth.

SOLUTION OF THE ENERGETIC COMPOUND

Q. I consider what has been said in relation to politics and science as relative and of secondary importance, at least for me. I recognise that every individual has the inevitable aim of re-discovering himself.

All social legislation is merely an attempt to harmonise the various conflicting *egos*. But there is no legislation and no political ideology which can give knowledge of the Self or knowledge of Being: they relate to the world of the individual which I wish to resolve and transcend. So, leaving the social problem to those who find it more congenial, I put this question to you: If through my will I inhibit one of my instinctive or emotional urges, and so on, because I see it to be absurd, what may be the psychological consequences? Bear in mind that within me there is awareness of the action and also a propensity to achieve an aim.

R. We have spoken at times about political issues, and politics operates at the level of becoming and contingency. Our problem here is to transcend becoming, and unless we set our sights on Being, we shall be unwittingly absorbed and involved in historical events. Being transcends history, and the Teaching is supra-historical but not anti-historical.

Being transcends time and space; it transcends process; and it transcends cause and effect.

Unless we keep our mind fixed on Being, we shall keep talking about temporal cycles, political history, economic ideologies, death and re-birth, and so on. The *jñānin* gathers the All into the eternal present, which is, in fact, outside time and space, cause and effect. I understand that your emotional sensitivity draws you towards the things that come and go, but I tell you to dare to look into your very own depths, fly towards your divine counterpart, rise up like the flight of the eagle above the historical, and you will attain the fullness of being. From this standpoint, or state of consciousness, you will be able to 'descend', and those who have the required qualifications and the responsibility of a universal *Dharma* will be able to build the traditional Society of being. We are also here for this purpose, but first of all we must acknowledge a Teaching which will lead us to distinguish between profane action and *action* which is in conformity with the intelligible world.

Let us examine our brother's question. Having spoken earlier about *artha* and *kāma*, we can now give a fuller answer. So let us take a step back: *dharma, artha, kāma* and *mokṣa* constitute the motivating aim and substratum of human behaviour, but into how many stages can we divide them?

The Philosophy of Being suggests that there are four stages, which represent precise *level of consciousness* for the individual: *Brahmacārin* (student), *Gṛhastha* (householder), *Vānaprastha* (contemplative anchorite), and *Saṁnyāsin* (renunciate). These stages are also known as *Āśramas*. I am using the Hindu terminology, but these things are above nationality.

Those who have a distaste for the East might dislike these terms, but I would ask you to transcend this. We need names to refer to specific experiences and ways of life. We are moving towards universality, and some languages use specific technical terms which others unfortunately do not have. Let us instead understand one another and not build up resistance against things of no importance. On the other hand, Philosophy as we understand it is not a story to be read in one's spare time.

So, the student stage is characterised by apprenticeship; the householder stage, by the sense of self-determination, responsibility for family and work, social relationships, and so on; that of the anchorite, by withdrawal into oneself, re-orientation of one's own energies, and the urge to get closer to *mokṣa*; and that of the renunciate, by detachment from the whole world of becoming. Now each stage of life involves a precise *dharma*, which means that the *dharma* of the student is not that of the householder, and so with the others. Let us say that each stage comprehends a precise experience of consciousness. Without going into detail, you can understand by yourselves the full implication and the harmony of the whole.

We must emphasise that, according to the Philosophy of Being, the individual – and therefore humanity – is here for a precise purpose: to *know himself, comprehend himself, be*. So the individual is not here in order to think of himself as a Prince, entrepreneur, or manual worker. He is not here to make money and accumulate wealth, resort to violence and copulate. His categorical imperative is, in fact, to re-discover himself as *totality* or unity, to leave behind the fragmentation and incompleteness in which he finds himself.

Fortunately, he is more than an aggregate of force/work or desire which tends to benumb. Unless we appreciate this, we shall not be able to understand why the Philosophy of Being conceives politics, religion, philosophy, and so on in a particular way. We would say that we would not be able to understand even the philosophy of Parmenides, Pythagoras, Plato, Plotinus, and so on.

We are not here to act and to draw limits around ourselves on the plane of becoming by producing another becoming/prison, but we are here to transcend becoming itself and to bring to an end our imprisoning movement by realising that we are 'the unmoving Mover'.

With reference to the various *āśramas* we should remember that in some of our writings it is possible to find 'stimuli' directed to the *Brahmacārin*, the *Gṛhastha*, the *Vānaprastha*, and the *Saṁnyāsin*.

In this way we can see that Metaphysics, or the Philosophy of Being, is not a utopia and doesn't involve contemplating the starry heavens or the clouds while waiting for some hidden bearded God to peep down upon us and lift us out of the mess we've got ourselves into.

Let us go back to the question and stay with two points: first, the energy compound is to be dealt with according to the specific stage of life because it is, in fact, subject to variation; second, it is not a question of inhibiting but of resolving the energies, as far as the way chosen by our brother could also go; where awareness, purpose, and intelligence are present, there is never any inhibition.

+ How can I find out which of these stages of life I am in? I assume that, in considering stages of consciousness, they don't necessarily accord with biological age.

R. Quite right. There is no doubt that certain things concern *sādhanā* or *paidéia*, as well as the direct relationship of disciple to teacher; a *sādhanā* cannot be practised in isolation, especially at the beginning, so that the disciple can be given appropriate directions.

Q. In this respect should sex energy be observed carefully?

R. I would say so. The issue of sex varies with psychological and physical age, according to whether it concerns a man or a woman, and according to the psycho-somatic make-up of the moment, the precise physiological and psychological needs, the functioning of some of the centres or *cakras* above the diaphragm, and so on.

+ Then the question of sex is not so simple as one might think. Some people dismiss the problem with a couple of words: you attain liberation through chastity or, conversely, you attain liberation by continually having sex. Some tantric ways prescribe this on the pretext of withholding the sperm.

R. Sex is part of the whole psycho-physiological and even spiritual context of the individual. Like everything, it is therefore an energy which is neither good nor bad. It has its precise function and it serves specific purposes.

Q. Can one follow certain cycles which are in keeping with nature itself, with the rhythm of cosmic life?

R. Certainly. In fact, sex should be understood, mastered, and given direction and rhythm: this is the sequence. At certain levels it can be transcended. The question of sex is approached intelligently not only by a particular kind of tantrism but also by every kind of *yoga*. Let us remember, however, that physiological sex represents a *symbol* of universal order.

Unfortunately, the symbol is often divested of its real meaning; hence the need for the proper appreciation which was referred to earlier.[1]

Q. Why is there so much emphasis on sex, at least here in the West?

R. You see, sexual energy, like the energy of *manas* (mind) and *kāma* (desire), although harmless in itself, can be used rightly or wrongly. Unfortunately, the individual has prostituted this symbol, as we were saying earlier, and deprived it of its deepest significance, and nowadays our use of sex has reached the point of being worse than that of animals. In fact, animals have precise biological rhythms which are safeguarded, apart from the fact that, not having the *imagination* or desire of speculation, they cannot anticipate it, as human beings do, especially in recent times.

Q. I believe that sex is definitely an individual matter. We cannot generalise or lay down common standards. Don't you think so?

R. I agree. As with all the other energies, it's necessary to examine the individual's level of consciousness.

---

[1] See 'Name, form and *vāsanā*' in *Beyond Doubt*, by Raphael. Aurea Vidyā, New York.

To speak in terms of biological age, a twenty-year-old may even try to transcend sex, for example, while for a forty-year-old it may not be appropriate yet to stop it completely. It also depends on the neophyte's intention.

Q. Some groups, wishing to demolish every institution of the past and not wishing to inhibit any energy within the individual, maintain that the best way to realisation is to plunge into the sea of experience and life. They would like to go back to the instinctive religion of primitive man. Do you think this is right?

R. Let's go beyond right and wrong. Let's say that some people cannot understand the fundamental problem and are seeking to release energies which are merely subconscious. This means that, instead of uniting with the super-consciousness, they are merging with the sub-consciousness, which represents the crystallised past. They want to demolish the external crystallised institutions and then become slaves of subconscious energy contents and complexes which are now institutionalised.

A preconception, of any nature and degree, is always an *institution* which is clamouring to be made manifest.

If we are talking of primordial people, when man was more divine than human (*satya-yuga*), then we are in agreement, but if we are talking of primordial people in the *history of the ego*, of the fallen and metallised individual (*kali-yuga*), then I would disagree.

One of the many dangers of drugs lies precisely in the fact that, in disinhibiting some of the protective psychical coverings, the consciousness sinks down into the 'underworld' without being prepared, but Illumination is not to be found in this realm. Drugs can give momentary greater awareness of particular factors of individuality, and can present an ego which is apparently stronger, more euphoric, more capable, more open, and more perceptive, but, I repeat, this is not a matter for the initiatory Way.

In any case, it seems reasonable to me that energies which have been inhibited for a long time should find intelligent expression. We have spoken of stages of life, and each stage has its precise expression of energy. But what counts most of all is to understand one's own constitution, not only that pertaining to the coarse physical body but also the constitution of one's wholeness.

What also needs to be considered is that nowadays many groups are reacting against an inhibiting set of morals which is no longer relevant. So they are looking for the realisation of the *ego*, a greater expression of freedom for the ego. For *Realisation*, it's not a question of disinhibiting sexual energy (this is the kind of energy that is usually referred to) or the psychical energy of self-assertion, and so on; and it's not a question of reacting indiscriminately to all forms of authority, although all of this may be given due consideration: but it is a question of having true urges to *transcend* the ego itself.

We need to distinguish between what may turn out to be a beneficial *therapy* at a psychological level and a precise initiatory or realisative *iter*, between what is merely a psychological sexual education – the best thing, especially at the present time – and a *polar solution*. Let us recall that *advaita* means 'non-duality'.

Q. I have been told to be passive, to surrender to the *guru*. Am I putting myself into a wrong frame of mind?

R. In all sincerity, it has to be said that there is nothing worse than a premature *surrender*. People often have a desire to effect a condition which is very advanced. They want to embrace the Divine by surrendering before they've even started.

An ascent has two phases: one of an active order, and the other not so much one of passivity, we would say, as of receptivity, conscious waiting, availability.

The work of transformation, attainment, control, and so on, is of an active, solar order; when the ego is put to silence, then the individual as such can no longer do anything. It is the universal which absorbs the particular; it is the supreme Light which is put into a condition to re-absorb the reflection; it is Being in itself which completely resolves its diffusing ray. Human reason, empirical rationality, may have its relative validity only at the individual level, so that it can never grasp Being.

If we begin to surrender before completing the task of resolving the ego, all we are doing is surrendering to the intermediate world, the world of the psyche, of shadows, ghosts, and mediumism. From this perspective, one becomes a passive object of some being, some idol, some psychic power.

Surrender is not an easy matter, although it may seem to be so. In fact, it is the last step that can be taken by a consciousness which has been brought to maturity in the fire of purification.

When the mind has reached its extreme limit of 'impossibility' in seeking, desiring, possessing, when every effort has ceased, then, like a ripe fruit, it yields without resistance, without hesitation, without regrets. In this surrender there is 'isolation' (*kaivalya*)[1] from what precedes and what follows. This suggests that the consciousness, being folded back upon itself, has ceased to have expectations, has ceased to move.

Many people are attached to the Teaching itself, to metaphysical concepts, to the working out of the Teaching; they are meticulously attentive to the ideas which they have to express, and so on. But if they have truly reached maturity, there comes a day when they have to surrender all the terminology of the Teaching and seek to understand, directly, the truth which the idea embodies. When one moves from concept to experience, formulas cease to be of use, and if one isn't ready to drop these supports, the mind desperately clutches hold of them, putting off that indispensable surrender which must take place when one wishes – in practice, not in theory – to cross the abyss.

Q. Many people approach the Philosophy of Being with their mind. Can't what we have said about politics and science happen to such people? I have to say that it happened to me, too, but I am rectifying my position.

R. It is true, profoundly true. It's not a question of being pessimistic, but in this field, too, most people objectivise that which should not be objectivised.

In truth, if many *gurus* – especially Eastern ones – insist on saying that the mind should not be used, that the mind should be killed, so that some disciples are taken to a state

---

[1] For a deeper understanding of this state, see *Kaivalya Upaniṣad* in *Five Upaniṣads* and *Kaivalya pāda* in Patañjali's *Yogadarśana*. Translation from the Sanskrit and commentary by Raphael. Aurea Vidyā, New York.

of stupidity, it is because they are giving warnings of the dangers of the mind, which can operate in the field of spiritual ascent as it does in the worldly field. Hence the radical change of route. We have to be careful, however: everything has to find its rightful place. The middle way is the way of wisdom.

It needs to be acknowledged that the mind can create for itself its own idol/divinity, its own idol/quality of goodness, brotherhood, and so on, while the consciousness remains unchanged. There are people who worship the *projection* of Love, of Knowledge, of Will, while their consciousness is neither loving nor athirst for knowledge, nor volitional.

As long as we create the *other*, we are creating idols and alienation. Only in the One-without-a-second is there reality and expression of reality. *You are That*, you are Being, but until one realises this state one needs to pay great attention because one can create substitutes, surrogates which undoubtedly delay the awareness of oneself as pure Being.[1]

Erudition is another great idol which has many worshippers and faithful followers. The erudite person thinks of being while he is not; and it is difficult to make him understand this because generally he is proud and critical, with a mind that is frequently over-stimulated. He holds in his hands an objective psychical power which he doesn't want to give up. Erudition provides security for the relative and limited ego.

---

[1] For a deeper understanding of an operative path based on this 'great statement' (*Mahāvākya*), with expressive indications suited to a receptive Western way, see *Tat Tvam Asi*, by Raphael. Aurea Vidyā, New York.

Q. I should like to put a question, but I don't know whether we are running late. However, I'll put it, and if there is no time, never mind!

For some time now there's been a problem which is closely connected with women. That is, there's the problem of women considered as objects by men or, better, by males.

The society of becoming seeks to resolve this problem in the way which suits it. But how does the Philosophy of Being see this question?

R. So young, and you are interested in such problems?

+ Perhaps it's just because I am a girl.

R. My dear, for the Philosophy of Being the problem doesn't exist because, by considering each individual as the threefold expression of body/soul/spirit – or, to use the terms of *Vedānta*: *sthūlaśarīra*, *jīva*, and *ātman* – it sets the relationship on a threefold existential level. In this way, the woman, like the man, in addition to being body is also soul/*jīva*, with its course and its level of consciousness, and at the level of soul physical polarities disappear.
You and I are two drops of the same ocean. Then at the level of being, we are the same Reality. If this vision is lived, things cannot help changing in the relationship between the sexes.

We would say that woman, like man, is soul-*jīva* rather than body. Moreover, according to the Philosophy of Being the direction for individualities is towards the attainment of Being/unity; thus it is a vertical direction, one of transcendence, not one of gratification and acquisition.

The Philosophy of Being is inherent in the Self. The philosophy of becoming is inherent in the grasping empirical ego, and since it conceives of being as mere body/ego, it cannot resolve the problem of the man/woman relationship.

At the level of the body, taken by itself, there are only instinct and physiological need. In a physical society – if you will excuse these terms – the only possible relationship is one of copulation, possession, and usefulness. At the physical level, as we know, it is impossible for two bodies to coalesce. It is at the level of soul that there can be fusion, and therefore love.

According to the Philosophy of Being, Love is a level of consciousness in which there is no ego. The orientation of the philosophy of becoming is horizontal, quantitative, expansive, and gratifying to the ego. This is what we see at the level of consumer goods and, unfortunately, it's also what we observe at the level of sex itself. Nowadays there is also a consumerism of sex which, sooner or later, cannot but result in saturation, weariness, and surfeit.

+ If I have understood properly, with the Philosophy of Being do physical problems become problems of the soul?

R. The philosophy of becoming thinks of the sexual instinct as the determining factor.

According to the Philosophy of Being, two individuals meet first of all at the level of the Soul. It is from this position that efforts are then made to co-ordinate, integrate, harmonise, and express instinct/feeling/thoughts. In other words, it's important to distinguish between coupling and *union*.¹

+ Does sexual violence exist because the philosophy of becoming is expressed through the ego?

R. Yes. Violence is the result of reaction, acquisition, possession. In love there is neither reaction nor acquisition, but giving, surrendering, and contemplating.

The society of becoming has no love, no relationship, no communication, because it is based on the separatist ego and its attributes.

Q. Patañjali's *Rājayoga* says that there are eight means for balancing the three *guṇas* and thus realising *kaivalya*. It is an empirical and experiential procedure which I am reflecting on. On the other hand, what is the use of *Asparśayoga*? What means does it employ for the realisation of *nirguṇa Brahman*? What is the difference between the *rāja-yogin* and the *jñānin*?

R. If you study and meditate on the *Aparokṣānubhūti*, you will find the means advocated by *advaita* for resolving the energy complex of the ego and thus for realising *Brahman*. Moreover, you will find in this book an exposition of the difference between the two methods.² However, there is no opposition between them. Their methods are different, but their common objective is *mokṣa*.

---

[1] For an exposition of this topic from the perspective of Tradition, see *The Science of Love*, by Raphael. Aurea Vidyā, New York.

[2] Śaṅkara, *Aparokṣānubhūti* (Self-realisation), translation from the Sanskrit and commentary by Raphael. Aurea Vidyā, New York.

Asparśa is a realisative metaphysics and it resorts to intuitive understanding to recognise reality. Someone who truly *knows* cannot but be. Knowledge, not erudition, is cathartic and transformative. If we can appreciate that the world of names and forms is nothing but evanescent phenomenon, we will detach ourselves from it because it is not that absolute reality which we are searching for. We have to realise Being in its *nirguṇa* aspect, which is the true and absolute constant. We can transcend whatever is not Being, because it is just a reflection of *māyā*. We would add that *Rājayoga* operates particularly through the will and effects a gradual transformation of the consciousness. *Asparśa* operates particularly through the sattvic *buddhi*, super-conscious intuition, to distinguish absolute Truth from untruth and thus to bring about an instantaneous realisation of Being in its unconditioned state.[1]

Svāmi Siddheśvarānanda writes:

'*Jñāna* represents pure knowledge, knowledge of the One-without-a-second. This does not involve a religious attitude because it excludes a priori every notion pertaining to the world of existences and differences. "The knowers of the Self look with an equal eye upon a *Brāhmaṇa* endowed with wisdom and humility, a cow, an elephant, a dog, and a *paria*" (*Bhagavadgītā*, V, 18).

'The *jñānin* unceasingly re-ascends to Being and does not abide in any of the "existents" (to use the existentialist word). All existents [states of consciousness] through which the mystic passes, all visions of God, all

---

[1] To go deeper into *Rājayoga*, *Jñānayoga* and *Asparśayoga*, see Raphael's works, *Tat Tvam Asi*, The *Pathway of Non-Duality*. Aurea Vidyā, and *Essence and Purpose of Yoga*, Elements Books. See also Patañjali's *Yogadarśana*, translation from the Sanskrit and commentary by Raphael. Aurea Vidyā, New York.

hearings of His words, and even beatification, are nothing but "existents", that is, projections through which Being is manifested, but they are not Being. For the *jñānin* who has realised Being, these are merely spectacles, *dṛṣya*, and they leave no mark upon him because he participates in that which is their true nature, in that single Being in which he himself is established."[1]

In our context, we should speak of Non-Being rather than Being, for Being is already a *determination*. But leaving aside metaphysical subtleties – which in any case have already been propounded elsewhere – we may nonetheless speak of Being, purely with reference to the Unconditioned.

If we also say 'Non-Being', this is not to negate Being, but because the *nirguṇa* Unconditioned can be comprehended only in terms of *'neti neti*: not this, not this', according to the direction of the *Upaniṣad*.

You know that *Advaita Vedānta* has two terms to designate the two aspects: *saguṇa Brahman*, or Being, and *nirguṇa Brahman* or Unconditioned Non-Being; or even the non-supreme *Brahman* and the supreme *Brahman*, but this is at the level of mere names.

The Western Tradition itself speaks, in different terms, of the state of Non-Being. Pythagoras, Parmenides, Plato, Plotinus, and others speak of the One or the supreme Unity (ἕν), which is even beyond *Noûs*, being, Plato's World of Ideas.[2]

---

[1] *Svāmi* Siddheśvarānanda, *Pensiero indiano e Mistica carmelitana*.

[2] See 'Parmenides and his Vision' in *The Pathway of Non-Duality*, by Raphael. Aurea Vidyā, New York.

Q. I have read many books on *yoga* and on *darśanas*. I have tried to penetrate the entire Teaching, and I have arrived at a synthesis which I have corroborated by studying and meditating on the *Asparśa* expounded in the *Māṇḍūkya Upaniṣad*.[1] I am happy to be in harmony with my intention. I think there is no higher expression than a *constant* which represents the unity and polar centre of everything manifest or unmanifest. I cannot conceive of a multiple Reality, and science itself has now come to acknowledge the unity of physical life.

For the past two years this vision has been close to me all the time. I recognise it to be always valid, and I am happy. However, every now and again I find that some of my attitudes are not truly consistent with this vision. So on the one hand I accept the *constant*, and I couldn't but affirm it; but on the other hand I can observe a psyche which lives a conditioned life, and this has reached a point where I wonder whether I have really comprehended, whether I have truly accepted this *constant*.

What is this thing within me which holds me within limits and the phenomenal world? What can I do to free myself from it?

R. For the moment, have no fear. This is a condition that is common to so many people.

We have often said that the Philosophy of Being is both practice and theory. These two aspects are not divided or in opposition. They are not two separate moments, but they interpenetrate each other, and this we mustn't forget.

---

[1] See the *Māṇḍūkyakārikā*. Translation from the Sanskrit and Commentary by Raphael. Aurea Vidyā, New York.

If one has a developed *buddhi* (intuition), and if one has a harmonised *manas* (discriminating mind), the theory can be easily grasped. But if there is no well-developed will or a strong thirst to *be* the vision, it may happen that the theory gets the upper hand over the practice, which is thus relegated to second place. This is the case with many *paṇḍits*, erudite people, cultured people, who, however much they know, in truth are not. If, on the other hand, one possesses great will-power, high aspirations, but a *buddhi* which is still quiescent, then one has an attitude of *doing*, of imposing upon oneself types of behaviour which are even psychological and of doing violence to oneself. But if the vision is not there, one can fall into many errors and even into perversions.

A self-imposed technicism without an intelligent vision can have far-reaching effects. Many psychical, mystical, emotional visionaries could leave behind their erroneous condition if they were to develop *manas* and *buddhi* sufficiently. So theory and practice are not separate; and where they are separate, there will necessarily be some deviation.

After this preamble defining the problem, let us examine the question more closely. What is this something which is constraining me?

When present-day consciousness appreciates certain truths, it obviously cannot disregard them and it seeks to assimilate them, but in translating them into practice it encounters resistances which, in spite of its strong determination, often make it deviate from the truth which it has glimpsed. The consciousness understands that it has to follow a prescribed way of behaviour, but a *certain something* which is within its psychical domain prevents it from doing so. The clinical picture - let us call that - appears to be like this. Is that how it seems to you?

+ Yes, I would say that this is the condition which I spoke about earlier.

R. Well, what is this something which prevents you from being what you would like to be? Some religions speak of a 'demon' which tries to carry the individual away from his path. Others speak of individual and universal evil, the power of constraining matter, *avidyā*, and so forth.
   Do you wish me to help you in this discussion?

+ Yes, certainly.

R. If you decided to get up tomorrow morning, let's say at four o'clock, what could oppose this conscious decision?

+ The pleasure of sleeping, staying in bed, mental inertia, which don't give me the strength to get up. That's how it seems to me.

R. So it's the pleasure of sleeping and idling about. Again if you decide to be nice to everyone, and then you stop being nice when something upsets you, what is it that has changed your attitude?

+ The ego's reaction. When particular things happen, subconscious mechanisms are triggered.

R. That's the key word: subconscious. So we don't need to go any further. We can stay with this word.

What do you generally understand by the sub-consciousness?

+ The sub-consciousness is the receptacle for our actions, our tendencies. It is our past.

R. So it is the summation of our tendencies. It is the crystallised *force* of our past. It is that part of you which moves as something reactive, instinctive, and automatic, because it is, in fact, the crystallisation of attitudes. It is an electronic brain which, if one of its keys is touched (reception of an impulse), responds automatically by producing the reaction by itself (response to the impulse). These crystallised attitudes are obviously constructions in time and space. Our habits are repeated attitudes which slowly crystallise, becoming, in fact, habits, customary ways: we would say, a *habitus*, an inurement. The animal is determined above all by subconscious impulse. The individual, by contrast, should be guided by intelligence. When receiving a stimulus, the animal responds automatically (conditioned reflex). Man ought to respond with intelligence, discrimination, and intuitive hyperconscious discernment.

It is important, therefore, to understand that the subconsciousness is the effect, the result, of a particular mental *direction* and a subsequent type of behaviour which slowly - through repeated expression - have taken hold of body, life, existence.[1]

Let's take an example: we are walking and we are faced by two roads which we shall call A and B (there may be other roads, however). *Today* we are free to take one or the other, so that we decide, in *freedom*, to walk along

---

[1] See 'The origin of sub-consciousness' in *Tat Tvam Asi*, by Raphael. Aurea Vidyā, New York.

road B. Since this road has found an adequate response in our consciousness, we continue to go along it every day, until the energy crystallises and gives shapes to a part of itself. It becomes accustomed to this occurrence and identified with it, forgetting the starting-point. At this stage a mechanism is triggered: the original *freedom* to decide is replaced by the need to undertake an action, the action of going along road B. Now the force of habit, like a drug, is impelling us to follow a *pre-determined* way. This is how our consciousness, originally free in its vital movement, has been *determined*, crystallised, constrained. In other words, it has *fallen* under the law of necessity and determination.

What can happen now to this consciousness which has been determined?

+ I am all ears. Something new is dawning inside me. I wouldn't want to interrupt.

R. Then let us proceed. As long as the consciousness is tuned to that vital expression, and in our case to that specific route, nothing happens. Everything goes forward under full sail. The journey seems beautiful, wonderful, and if anyone upsets it or spoils it, or even *begins* to suggest that it is not suitable, we defend it and say that this person understands nothing and doesn't live in the real world (route B), is a poor old fellow that one should feel sorry for; and if he insists and tries to prove what he says, we shall use all our resources to repulse him and, in an extreme case, to shut him up in a mental home.

Let us consider that we ourselves are the ones who are awaking. And so what can happen as a result of our urge to awake? Two things: in time and space the obstacles (pain) which appear before us are so numerous and of such a nature that we begin to get glimmers of a suspicion that something isn't going our way. Slowly the barriers push us back, make us return into ourselves, make us reflect, and this drives us towards the *source* from which we started as *free* agents; that is, it drives us towards the starting-point (an inevitable necessity, because the centre/consciousness always tends to reprise its original position; thus the uneasiness of the individual is born, in fact, from losing the central reference point). Or again it may happen - and this is more difficult – that an act of immediate awareness, of total comprehension, causes us to recognise that we are proceeding in a way that is mistaken, if not totally, then at least partially.

It is only during this phase of *acknowledgement* that the consciousness is ready to listen, to be humbler in its declarations, more disposed towards realisation, and not earlier.

If you were to go to a philosophical gathering to preach road A, C, or D, when the members of the gathering acknowledge only road B and are proud and enthusiastic about it, you would come out in tatters. Let's say you were prompted to speak by your irresponsibility, or your conscious courage, or your 'mission', which could, however, lead to tragic results. The ones who think differently from the current general *opinion* know something about this.

Let us now admit that there has been an awakening within our consciousness and that we have had the proper vision. It is obvious that at this point the consciousness wills *to be* that vision, but in effecting this, one becomes aware of some resistances, some forces of inertia which impel it to take the habitual road and repeat the behaviour.

Let us go back to the question: What constricts us? I think we now have a clear answer: What constricts us is unconscious, automatic habit, assimilation to road B, consolidated *force*. In other words, it is one part of *our* consciousness which is working in opposition to another part (the birth of duality).

The demon, the devil, and so on, turn out to be us ourselves, a part of our consciousness; they are not outside us, but inside, deep inside, nestled within us and so well cultivated that, as powerful operating forces, they seek to restrict the free will of the awakened being. This is why we were saying some days ago that politics, working from outside, cannot restore peace, justice, and harmony among individuals.

Now, how can the freedom which has been lost be regained? How can habits going back to the dawn of time be eliminated? How can we come out of a world of restrictions, conflict, suffering, duality and unilateralness? How can we return to the point at the centre, to the *origin*, the primordial state, the pure state, the state of the Garden of Eden, and so on, according to the various descriptions given by the Philosophy of Being?

Thus arises *sādhanā*, which represents the return journey, the integration of theory and practice, the ascent back to freedom, back to the starting point. Needless to say, all of this also shows that the individual is not an 'evolute' but an 'involute' and that his immediate task is to 'awaken' to what he truly is.

Initiation consists in sowing the seed of awakening in *the soil that has been prepared* and qualified; but it is up to the disciple to bring it to maturity.

Sādhanā represents precisely this concrete act, this way of effective realisation. This is the philosophical Ascent.

Q. My perception is that when I was free to decide, I could choose one of a number of roads. I wonder who made me take this particular road. I realise that I have taken the wrong road. On the other hand, things fall into place. Years ago I was free to make certain decisions rather than others; or rather, I should say that I was free not to take any at all, and I wish I had not taken any! Well, I made a decision which later brought me great suffering and imprisoned me. Even now I am still undergoing the consequences. Please excuse the expression, but I have often cursed the moment I made that decision.

Can I get out of this path of suffering and at last find peace on my own?

R. I understand the level of consciousness of someone who is in the process of awakening to the recognition that we are not road B. I also understand the feelings which often come into play with particular reactions. But we must try to have an even better comprehension and *be* that comprehension.

We can say some things in relation to your question. First of all, one transcends a road only after assimilating and exhausting it. So an experience becomes absurd only when it has been transcended, when there is no longer any response to it.

Road B – just to return to our example – went well for us at the beginning; otherwise, we would have changed it at the right moment, that is, when we were no longer able to walk along it in complete tranquillity. Beware, then, because today you do not find peace from having travelled along a road which you consider to be wrong, but I ask you to take note of the word 'today'. The mistake, then, is not in walking along road B, but *in assimilating* the consciousness to this road, in creating a sub-consciousness, in crystallising the event as if it were absolute. The mistake lies in *getting lost* in the particular.

One who is realised is not one who shuns the various roads. If he thinks it right, he may also follow them, but he is not identified with them, he doesn't get lost in them, he doesn't annihilate himself in them, and he doesn't create a sub-consciousness. Thus he is free of the laws which create necessity.

+ Do you mean being in the world but not of the world?

R. Exactly. This is the optimal condition of someone who experiences without experiencing.[1] The *Bhagavadgītā* speaks of action without action.

Forgive me if I insist on this, but I'm doing so because many of you, especially at the beginning of *sādhanā*, wear your brains out in trying to understand the *reason* for the 'fall'. In simple terms, we fell because we wanted to fall. The Being is free to be or not to be.[2]

---

[1] See 'Being in the world but not of the world' in *Tat Tvam Asi*, by Raphael. Aurea Vidyā, New York.

[2] See 'The fall of the Soul' in *The Pathway of Non-Duality*, by Raphael. Aurea Vidyā, New York.

Q. Was I able, for example, to take roads A, C, or D?

R. Yes. No one forced us to take one road rather than another, just as no one is forcing us to remain on the same road. The world of names and forms is nothing but a proliferation of living expressions (roads). One of these is, in fact, the human expression. No one has forced us to travel the way of human beings, except our own free choice (free will). On the other hand, we cannot say that the way of human beings is better or worse, higher or lower, than any other. It is one way amongst the multitudinous ways, and that's all we can say. It can improve or deteriorate, according to our response and the direction of energy that we impart to our actions.

I would say that we are mistaken even when we express ourselves in terms of super-human and sub-human, especially when we are referring to ethical aspects of manasic superiority or inferiority, and so on. Every road, or expression of life, has its idiosyncrasies, which make it what it is. We could not add anything further; if we did, we would be impelled by the desire to assign to one expression of life the attributes pertaining to another: but this is not in conformity with reason. The earth is understood and studied from the viewpoint of its earthly nature, not from the viewpoint of Sirius or Vega.

Q. What you are saying seems right, at least to me. At the beginning I, too, was agonising over why I am here. Today I have transcended this question, and I admit that I can go away from here with the same freedom with which I decided to come. Fundamentally, that freedom, or autonomy, has not been destroyed but weakened, obfuscated, by identification with the part: here are the concepts of *māyā* and *avidyā* which cover and veil our free consciousness. Do correct me if I am wrong.

I should now like to know whether *nirguṇa* is that condition in which one remains aloof from all possible roads.

R. You are saying some interesting things. I hope that everyone has heard them.

Although the sub-consciousness, now crystallised and inert, can play some 'tricks', there is no obstacle that can prevail against an awakened consciousness, a will that has contemplated Being. The *nirguṇa* condition is the one that you have referred to.

At the beginning we find ourselves in the unmanifest, and therefore beyond all possible modes of manifestation (the different roads or pathways, and so on), and we can also remain in this state if we wish to. In other words, we are free not only to take one or other of the manifested roads, but also not to take any of them. We can call this last possibility 'Point X'.

You see, a little while ago our friend said some important things which may help us to comprehend what we are maintaining. He said that he had freedom of choice, or rather, he was absolutely free not to make any choice and thus remain at peace in his original state. This is our twofold possibility: to remain *nirguṇa*, 'Point X', or to experience A, B, C, and so on, in accordance with our particular direction. It is obvious that we cannot live two expressions of life simultaneously. A determination is a determination, a particularity.

Asparśayoga and *Advaita Vedānta* are those return pathways which lead to the Unconditioned, to pure, unlimited Being. They are pathways which are completely resolutive, metaphysical, because they pertain, in fact, to the Unmanifest, the supreme Reality which is not subject to change. This is the One-Good of Plato, the Being of Parmenides, the One of Plotinus.

According to the metaphysical *Asparśa*, the name 'absolute Reality' can be given only to the *nirguṇa*, attributeless *Brahman*, 'Point X' in our example, for all other possibilities are merely its spatio-temporal *determinations*. Of course, this type of *yoga*, having such a high and resolutive goal, is for the few, and Gauḍapāda himself says that many *yogis* flee in terror at the thought of losing themselves; so they are afraid of extinguishing the ego, that is, the individuality in its various ramifications. *Asparśa* means 'without support', 'without relationship', 'without contact', because *Brahman nirguṇa*, being the Absolute, has no relationship with anything. From this comes the expression 'Unity without a second'.[1]

Q. Could you give me a thumbnail sketch of the standpoints of consciousness relating to these roads, so that I might have a seed-form on which to meditate?

R. 'I am this' (*this* represents one of the roads). 'I am' (represents the being in its principial, a-formal state). The third stage represents pure Consciousness in its undetermined state, devoid therefore of even the determination[2]

---

[1] *Māṇḍūkyakārikā*, II, 39.

[2] Determination: 4. the determining of bounds; delimitation; definition 1594; The Shorter Oxford English Dictionary, Vol. I. Clarendon Press, Oxford.

of 'I am' as being which reflects itself: it remains *Turīya* alone, That.¹

Q. This static condition is still inconceivable to me, if I think that in front of me there is life, which is dynamism, movement, *pathos*, pulsating and full of feeling.

R. Indeed, some philosophers reject unmanifest Reality because they view it as cold, static, lifeless, and so forth. This shows, as we suggested earlier, that one is trying to judge one existential position against the paradigms of another existential position; or rather, by experiencing one polarity of life and being assimilated to this polarity, one isn't capable of comprehending any others. You see, for us human beings, the monotonous fluttering of the swallows may constitute something absurd, nonsensical, excessive, deranged; but you can be assured that the swallows will have very different ideas.

Q. You spoke earlier of a return to the Centre, to the state of the Garden of Eden, and so forth. I draw my inspiration from the Christian teaching, and I should like to know whether that original Centre represents Adam before the 'fall', and whether the various roads which you have portrayed represent the Tree of Good and Evil. If you could enlighten me on this point I would be able to have a better appreciation of what we have said.

R. Yes, it's the same thing. Adam, having fallen onto the plane of differentiation, must re-direct himself towards the

---

[1] For this succession, see 'Birth of energy coagulates' in *Beyond the Illusion of the Ego*, by Raphael. Aurea Vidyā, New York.

nature of Being. The various roads represent the endless possibilities which the Tree of Good and Evil (duality) has to offer.

Q. Today I see with greater clarity that only Knowledge effects a true catharsis, only Knowledge shows me the direction I have to take to attain Being.

In times past, *dialectic* was the art of reaching and gathering what is true by means of dialogue with oneself or others. Plotinus puts in first place this type of *dialectic*, that is, philosophy. Plato says, 'One who knows how to question and reply, what shall we call him if not a dialectician?'

For me there is no other way than that of realisative philosophy or effective dialectic, but I have been given to understand that *surrender* to Īśvara, to Śiva, and so on, also leads to liberation. Patañjali, too, speaks of this condition in some of his *sūtras*.[1]

I wonder: how can *surrender* to Īśvara represent a way back if one doesn't have the consciousness of knowing?

R. You may have been absent. We have already answered this question. However, we shall attempt to complete the picture that we gave previously.

Surrender is twofold: it can be to the world of becoming or to the world of Being.

If you surrender to the world of becoming, you are following the line of least resistance; you shouldn't have any psychological inhibitions; you plunge into the life of form (from this come the different psychologies which seek to 'liberate' the various instinctual processes); you

---
[1] *Yogadarśana*, I, 23; II, 1, 32, 45.

are born, you love, you hate, you copulate, you practise sport or politics or charity, and so on. In other words, you surrender to the world of instinct, emotion, and imagination. Instead of living, you allow yourself to be lived. Instead of thinking and planning, you are thought. If I am not mistaken, this is what existentialist philosophy aims at; this is its approach.

If becoming were absolute reality, this approach would be the wisest, apart from being the source of bliss. But since formal becoming is not absolute reality, then yielding to it means living under the rule of relativity, surrendering to the world of necessity, and necessity is constriction, and conflict, sooner or later. Let us say that becoming does not lead to Being. Realisation is not a matter of evolution in the course of time.

If, on the other hand, the surrender is with respect to being, then things change. The line of least resistance is replaced by that of greatest resistance; surrender to desire/ instinct and so on is replaced by surrender to the absence of desire.

Q. But this is a way of sacrifice, not a way of joyful surrender. By contrast, surrender to *Iśvara* or *Śiva* is motivated by joy.

R. Then we must say that there is joy and gladness where there is love.

If you love *Śiva* more than yourself (as an individuality), the ego dies sweetly. An ardent and impassioned heart, a heart overflowing with love, is where the beloved abides. If you succeed in loving Being more than yourself, you will so unite with it as to become Being.

Under the law of Love every death is life, every sacrifice is gain, every action or gesture is an offering. When you unite with the Beloved, who transcends the contingent, the world of becoming vanishes completely and loses all consistency, value, and meaning. We would say that you don't even see it. This is the true concept of 'Sacrifice'. The *Song of Songs* has something to teach us.

Of course, we are speaking of love that is conscious, intelligent, all-embracing, and not of love that is blind and deaf, that numbs the mind and the heart itself, instead of opening them. In most cases, love is numb and unintelligent, because it is self-love.

Individuality loves itself and sees in others only the object of its fulfilment, its compensation, its enjoyment, from which comes the subjugation of the object, ownership of the object. The ego is a monster of greed, and at times it appears with the face of an angel in order to destroy its victim more easily.

So in answer to our friend's question, we shall say that if in the surrender there is neither love nor proper knowledge of the Beloved, such a surrender may be dangerous. At the level of Love the emotions need to be purified; at the level of Knowledge the mind needs to be purified; at the level of Will desire needs to be purified.

Without proper purification and an intelligent *sādhanā*, conceptual games and philosophical sophism can occur in the sphere of the mind; in the sphere of feeling, visionary mysticism and emotional fanaticism; in the sphere of the will, self-assertive, exclusivist and destructive self-assertion.

Q. Since individuality is expressed in a threefold way, can it not use all three of its expressive aspects?

R. Yes, certainly. We would say that it never operates on just one line. But it may come about that the original urge, which determines the outcome, begins from one of the three aspects: love involves knowledge and will, knowledge involves love and will, and so forth.

The three aspects are not sundered; individuality itself is not in watertight compartments. On the contrary, we may state that any knowledge unaccompanied by love is deficient. Knowledge accompanied by love conveys wisdom. Wisdom, characterised by will, moves from the abstract to the concrete, from potency to act.

GLOSSARY

adharma: not conformable to *dharma*, that which violates the universal Order or the Law (*dharma*).

advaita: Non-duality; without a second, without duality.

Agni: the Vedic Divinity of Fire.

ahaṁkāra: literally, 'that which the ego does', or the 'sense of the ego'. It is associated with *manas* (the distinguishing/analytical empirical mind) and with *citta* (the repository of subconscious latent impressions).

artha: object; wealth and prosperity; one of the four aims of human existence.

asparśa: without contact, without relationship, without support.

Asparśavāda: the doctrine of 'no contact'.

asparśayoga: the yoga of 'no support'.

asparśin: one who has realised *asparśayoga*.

āśram: place where a spiritual discipline is practised.

ātman: the Self, Spirit, pure Consciousness, the Absolute within us.

avidyā: non-knowledge, metaphysical ignorance.

Bhagavadgītā : poetical and philosophical work which, together with the classical *Upaniṣads* and the *Brahmasūtra*, constitute the Threefold Science of *Vedānta*.

bhūta: primal elements of nature; primordial element.

Brahmā: principle manifesting the universe, related to the preserving principle (*Viṣṇu*) and the transforming principle (*Śiva*).

Brahmacārin: one who is living the student state (*āśrama*).

Brahman: absolute Reality, the Absolute in itself; 'That' (*Tat*); the One-without-a-second.

Brāhmaṇa: the first of the four traditional social orders (*varṇa*), the priestly order.

Brahman nirguṇa: *Brahman* without attributes or qualifications; Absolute.

Brahman saguṇa: *Brahman* with attributes; qualified Being; the God Person.

Bṛhadāraṇyaka Upaniṣad: one of the oldest and most important of the Vedic *Upaniṣads*. It contains one of the four 'great sayings' in the *Upaniṣads*: *ahaṁ brahmāsm*i (I am *Brahman*).

buddhi: higher intellect, intuition, discriminating knowledge.

cakra: wheel, circle, centre, plexus. Seven principal *cakras* are recognised, situated along the length of the spine, from the coccyx right up to the top of the head.

daimon: literally, 'demon'; soul, life-aspect.

darśana: 'point of view', view, prospect. The term is applied in particular to the six orthodox schools of

Hindu philosophy: *Sāṁkhya*, *Yoga*, *Nyāya*, *Vaiśeṣika*, *Pūrva Mīmāṁsā*, and *Vedānta*.

dharma: Law, universal Order/Harmony; conformity to the Principle. One of the four goals of human existence.

diánoia: the selective, analytical, empirical mind, corresponding to *manas*.

dīkṣā: initiation, consecration.

dṛśya: 'spectacle', manifestation.

éthos: ethics.

Gauḍapāda: author of the *Māṇḍūkyakārikā*, a verse commentary (*kārikā*) on the *Māṇḍūkya Upaniṣad*, where he expounds *ajātivāda* (the doctrine of non-generation, non-creation) and *asparśayoga* (the *yoga* of 'no support'). The spiritual Teacher of Śaṅkara.

Gṛhastha: one who is living the state of householder.

guṇa: principial attributes, qualitative principles of *prakṛti*/universal substance. There are three: *tamas* (inertia), *rajas* (activity), *sattva* (equilibrium, harmonious rhythm).

guru: Instructor, spiritual master.

Īśvara: universal Being, principle of every manifestation, corresponding to the *Brahman* with attributes (*saguṇa*).

jīva: living being, individualised soul.

jñānin: knower; one who practises *jñānayoga*; one who has reached ultimate Knowledge (*paravidyā*).

kaivalya: absoluteness, the state of isolated unity; absolute unity (Non-duality).

kali-yuga: the dark age, also called the iron age; the fourth of the four *yugas* (eras).

kāma: desire, attachment to the sensory world. One of the four goals of human existence.

kāma/manas: the sensory mind/desire; the chief characteristic of human individuality.

kārikā: verse; verse commentary; compact exposition in verse of a philosophical teaching, ritual, and so on.

Kaṭha Upaniṣad: one of the oldest *Upaniṣads*, based on the dialogue between the young Naciketas and Yama, the god of death, who reveals to him the destiny of man after the death of the body, and thus his immortal nature.

Kṣatriya: the second of the four social orders, that of the lawgivers and warriors, corresponding to the Guardians of Plato's *Politéia*.

manas: the selective, analytical, empirical mind (see also *diánoia*).

manasic: related to *manas*.

maṇḍala: circle, wheel; disc; a support for certain types of meditation.

Māṇḍūkyakārikā: verse commentary (*kārikā*) by Gauḍapāda on the *Māṇḍūkya Upaniṣad*.

mantra: sacred formula or word for concentration or meditation; vibrant thought.

māyā: appearance/phenomenon; the empirical phenomenal world; all that constitutes a modification (*upādhi*) superimposed on the pure Consciousness of the *ātman*/Self.

mokṣa: liberation, emancipation from the becoming/relative, liberation from *avidyā* or *māyā* and from the subsequent transmigratory becoming (*saṁsāra*). One of the four goals of human existence.

neti neti: 'not this, not this'. Negating formula by which the *jñānin* discards, piece by piece, everything that is appearance in order to eventually reach the sole reality, *Brahman*.

nirguṇa: without attributes, unqualified, Absolute. See *Brahman nirguṇa*.

nirvāṇa: extinction, turning off, dissolving. Supreme state in which the individual (separate) aspect of the being has disappeared, to be replaced by the consciousness of Reality.

noésis: activity of the *noûs*, noetic thought, whose object is the intelligible. Corresponds to the *buddhi*.

non-duality: see *advaita*.

noumenon: relates to the *noûs* as pure intellect.

noûs: pure intellect.

'dós: Way, path, corresponding to *sādhanā* or spiritual practice.

paidéia: literally, education; spiritual ascent.

paṇḍit: learned, erudite.

politéia: literally, 'constitution'. Plato's fundamental work, usually translated as 'The Republic'.

prāṇa: vital breath or energy; that which provides energy for the maintenance of the gross/physical body.

Qabbālāh: literally, 'transmission', 'reception'; the esoteric Teaching of the Old Testament.

rājayogin: one who practises *Rājayoga*.

sādhanā: practice or discipline for spiritual elevation; ascent, or spiritual effort.

saguṇa: with attributes, qualified; refers to the *Brahman* endowed with attributes (*guṇas*). The equivalent of *Īśvara*. See *Brahman saguṇa*.

Śakti: dynamic energy, potentiality of *māyā*, the energy of the manifestation.

samādhi: etymologically, *samādhi* means transcendent identity. Contemplation.

Sāṁkhya: name of one of the oldest Brahmanical *darśana*s, which contemplates the thesis of a dualistic realism whose principal manifesting poles are *puruṣa* and *prakṛti*

Saṁnyāsin: ascetic renunciate; one who, having 'comprehended', has renounced everything.

saṁsāra: non-ending cycle of becoming; transmigratory becoming as a continuous passage through different levels of consciousness and thus of existence; transmigration.

Śaṅkara: the codifier of *Advaita Vedānta*, the metaphysical *darśana* which transcends religious duality and ontological monism. One of the greatest knowers/philosophers of all time, Śaṅkara is considered by many to be a philosopher, a mystic, an exegete of the *Śruti*, a founder of monastic orders and monasteries (*maṭha*), a national hero, the supreme Teacher (*ācārya*) who was able to point out the true supreme goal of human existence: the recognition of our real nature and liberation from the world of becoming/*saṁsāra*.

satya-yuga: the age of gold, the first of the four *yugas*.

Śiva: the Beneficent; one of the three aspects of the Divine, the aspect which transforms and dissolves.

Śruti: hearing; the 'heard' Tradition; sacred Knowledge as 'immediately' revealed (*Veda*).

sthūlaśarīra: the gross body.

Śūdra: the fourth of the traditional orders of society, the order of manual workers.

sūtra: a pithy statement in which an aspect of a work or a teaching is concisely expressed.

Svāmi: monk; also Teacher/Master.

télos: end, purpose, goal.

theoria: contemplation; corresponds to *samādhi*.

Turīya: the 'Fourth', the Absolute, *nirguṇa Brahman*.

upādhi: superimposition; that which is superimposed on the Self, becoming its expressive, but also limiting, 'vehicle'.

Upaniṣad: 'esoteric sessions or teachings'. It signifies sitting beside the Master to hear his words.

Vaiśya: the third of the four traditional orders of society, the class producing wealth.

Vānaprastha: hermit, anchorite.

Vedānta: the fulfilment of the *Vedas*. It is one of the six *darśana*s and is also called *Uttara Mīmāṁsā*.

Vedānta Advaita: non-dual *Vedānta*, codified by Gauḍapāda and Śaṅkara. As a non-dual teaching or 'viewpoint', it is not opposed to the other *darśanas* but comprehends and transcends them.

vidyā: knowledge; knowledge of Reality; conscious meditation leading to Realisation.

Viṣṇu: one of the three aspects of the Hindu *Trimurti*; the Divine considered particularly under the aspect of the preservation of the creation.

RAPHAEL

Unity of Tradition

Raphael having attained a synthesis of Knowledge (which is not to be associated with eclecticism or with syncretism) aims at 'presenting' the Universal Tradition in its many Eastern and Western expressions. He has spent a substantial number of years writing and publishing books on the spiritual experience; his works include commentaries on the *Qabbālāh*, Hermeticism, and Alchemy. He has also commented on and compared the Orphic Tradition with the works of Plato, Parmenides, and Plotinus. Furthermore, Raphael is the author of several books on the pathway of non-duality (*Advaita*), which he has translated from the original Sanskrit, offering commentaries on a number of key Vedāntic texts.

With reference to Platonism, Raphael has highlighted the fact that, if we were to draw a parallel between Śaṅkara's *Advaita Vedānta* and a Traditional Western Philosophical Vision, we could refer to the Vision presented by Plato. Drawing such a parallel does not imply a search for reciprocal influences, but rather it points to something of paramount importance: a single Truth, inherent in the doctrines (teachings) of several great thinkers, who, although far apart in time and space, have reached similar and in some cases even identical conclusions.

One notices how Raphael's writings aim to manifest and underscore the Unity of Tradition from the metaphysical perspective. This does not mean that he is in opposition to a dualistic perspective, or to the various religious faiths or 'points of view'.

An embodied real metaphysical Vision cannot be opposed to anything. What counts for Raphael is the unveiling, through living and being, of that level of Truth which one has been able to contemplate.

In the light of the Unity of Tradition Raphael's writings or commentaries offer to the intuition of the reader precise points of correspondence between Eastern and Western Teachings. These points of reference are useful for those who want to address a comparative doctrinal study and to enter the spirit of the Unity of Teaching.

For those who follow either the Eastern or the Western traditional line these correspondences help in comprehending how the *Philosophia Perennis* (Universal Tradition), which has no history and has not been formulated by human minds as such, 'comprehends universal truths that do not belong to any people or any age'. It is only for lack of 'comprehension' or 'synthetic vision' that one particular Branch is considered the only reliable one. From this position there can be only opposition and fanaticism. What degrades the Teaching is sentimental, fanatical devotionalism as well as proud intellectualism, which is critical and sterile, dogmatic and separative.

In Raphael's words: 'For those of us who aim at Realisation, it is our task is to get to the essence of every Teaching, because we know that, just as Truth is one, so Tradition is one even if, just like Truth, Tradition may be viewed from a plurality of apparently different points of view. We must abandon all disquisitions concerning the phenomenal process of becoming, and move onto the plane of Being. In other words, we must have a Philosophy of Being as the foundation of our search and our realisation'.[1]

Raphael interprets spiritual practice as a 'Path of Fire'. Here is what he writes: 'The "Path of Fire" is the pathway each disciple follows in all branches of the Tradition; it is the Way of Return. Therefore, it is not the particular teaching of an individual nor a path parallel to the one and only Main Road... After all, every disciple follows his own "Path of Fire", no matter which Branch of the Tradition he belongs to'.

In Raphael's view, what is important is to express through living and being the truth that one has been able to contemplate. Thus, for each being, one's expression of thought and action must be coherent and in agreement with one's own specific *dharma*.

After more than 60 years of teaching, both oral and written, Raphael has withdrawn into the *mahāsamādhi*.

* * *

May Raphael's Consciousness, expression of Unity of Tradition, guide and illumine along this Opus all those who donate their *mens informalis* (non-formal mind) to the attainment of the highest known Realization.

---

[1] See Raphael, *Tat tvam asi*, (That thou art). Aurea Vidyā, New York

PUBLICATIONS

Aurea Vidyā Collection

1. Raphael, *The Threefold Pathway of Fire*, Thoughts that Vibrate for an Alchemical, Æsthetical, and Metaphysical ascesis
ISBN 978-1-931406-00-0

2. Raphael, *At the Source of Life*, Questions and Answers concerning the Ultimate Reality
ISBN 978-1-931406-01-7

3. Raphael, *Beyond the illusion of the ego*, Synthesis of a Realizative Process
ISBN 978-1-931406-03-1

4. Raphael, *Tat tvam asi*, That thou art, The Path of Fire According to the Asparśavāda
ISBN 978-1-931406-12-3

5. Gauḍapāda, *Māṇḍūkyakārikā*, The Metaphysical Path of Vedānta*
ISBN 978-1-931406-04-8

6. Raphael, *Orphism and the Initiatory Tradition*
ISBN 978-1-931406-05-5

7. Śaṅkara, *Ātmabodha*, Self-knowledge*
ISBN 978-1-931406-06-2

8. Raphael, *Initiation into the Philosophy of Plato*
   ISBN 978-1-931406-07-9

9. Śaṅkara, *Vivekacūḍāmaṇi*, The Crest-jewel of Discernment*
   ISBN 978-1-931406-08-6

10. *Dṛdṛśyaviveka*, Discernment between *ātman* and non-*ātman*. Attributed to Śaṅkara*
    ISBN 978-1-931406-09-3

11. Parmenides, *On the Order of Nature*, Περί φύσεως, For a Philosophical Ascesis*
    ISBN 978-1-931406-10-9

12. Raphael, *The Science of Love*, From the desire of the senses to the Intellect of Love.
    ISBN 978-1-931406-12-3

13. Vyāsa, *Bhagavadgītā*, The Celestial Song*
    ISBN 978-1-931406-13-0

14. Raphael, *The Pathway of Fire according to the Qabbālāh* (Ehjeh 'Ašer 'Ehjeh), I am That I am.
    ISBN 978-1-931406-14-7

15. Patañjali, *The Regal Way to Realization*, Yogadarśana*
    ISBN 978-1-931406-15-4

16. Raphael, *Beyond Doubt*, Approaches to Non-duality
    ISBN 978-1-931406-16-1

17. Bādarāyaṇa, *Brahmasūtra*
    ISBN 978-1-931406-17-8

18. Śaṅkara, *Aparokṣānubhūti*, Self-realization*
    ISBN 978-1-931406-19-2

19. Raphael, *The Pathway of Non-Duality*
    ISBN 978-1-931406-21-5

20. *Five Upaniṣads**, Īśa, Kaivalya, Sarvasāra, Amṛtabindu, Atharvaśira
ISBN 978-1-931406-26-0

21. Raphael, *The Philosophy of Being*
ISBN 978-1-931406-27-7

Related Publications

Raphael, *Essence and Purpose of Yoga*, The Initiatory Pathways to the Transcendent
Element Books, Shaftesbury, U.K.
ISBN 978-1-852308-66-7

Śaṅkara, *A brief biography*
Aurea Vidya. New York.
ISBN 978-1-931406-11-6

Forthcoming Publications

Śaṅkara, *Brief Works,** Treatises and Hymns

Raphael, *Awakening*

Māṇḍūkya Upaniṣad, with the Gauḍapāda's *kārikās* and the Commentary of Śaṅkara

Upaniṣads*

Raphael, *Essence and Purpose of Yoga*, The Initiatory Pathways to the Transcendent

* Translation from Sanskrit or Greek and Commentary by Raphael.

Aurea Vidyā is the Publishing House of the Parmenides Traditional Philosophy Foundation, a Not-for-Profit Organization whose purpose is to make Perennial Philosophy accessible.

The Foundation goes about its purpose in a number of ways: by publishing and distributing Traditional Philosophy texts with Aurea Vidyā, by offering individual and group encounters, by providing a Reading Room and daily Meditations, at its Center.

* * *

Those readers who have an interest in Traditional Philosophy are welcome to contact the Foundation at: parmenides.foundation@earthlink.net.

www.ingramcontent.com/pod-product-compliance
Lightning Source LLC
Chambersburg PA
CBHW020754160426
43192CB00006B/328